I0150668

Life Behind Bars

An Irreverent Guide
to the Restaurant Industry

Other Books From
LAST CALL PRESS

The Frankie McKeller Mystery Series:

Murder in Myrtle Beach

The Ocean Forest
By Troy D. Nooe

Damn Yankee
By Troy D. Nooe

Long-Legged Rosie
By Troy D. Nooe

Five Kinds of Nothing
(ebook exclusive)
By Troy D. Nooe

LIFE BEHIND
BARS

AN IRREVERENT GUIDE
TO THE RESTAURANT INDUSTRY

By
C.J. Spaulding

Last Call
PRESS

Last Call Press

Myrtle Beach, South Carolina

Copyright © Troy D. Nooe

Cover Art by Samantha Gustafson

Photo by Matt Keskin

Logo by Matt Thomas

Edited by Caroline P. Smith

ISBN-13: 978-0692712054

ISBN 10: 0692712054

Dedicated to all the freaks, misfits, and miscreants

I've worked alongside over the years.

Without you, this book wouldn't be.

Give a man a fish and feed him for a day.
Put him in a fish suit and stick him in front of
a Long John Silvers, then you've really got something.

C.J. Spaulding

CONTENTS

INTRODUCTION

This book started off as a lark. Originally, it was a written two pages at a time, a goofy diversion to make my coworkers laugh. Somehow, it grew from there.

Before I knew it, people were coming out of the woodwork to give opinions and share stories. Many hours were logged sitting in some random bar, swapping horror stories and anecdotes.

If you are one of the people who shared a story with me and it didn't make it into the book, I apologize. If you are a person who shared a story and it did make it into the book, I apologize more. It means I blatantly took your story for my own means, giving you no credit whatsoever. I'm a jerk like that.

If I were to claim that this book was ten years in the making, it wouldn't be a complete lie. Sure, for most of those ten years, it sat in a desk drawer, but what does that matter?

When I took it out, after all that time, it was, again, to pass around work and make my coworkers laugh. They are the people who inspired me to get back to work on it and to turn it into something viable. I can't thank them enough.

I should warn you, this is not the end-all book on bartending and serving. It wasn't meant to be.

There is something else that goes along with working in the restaurant business. It's a certain sense of humor, a slanted and sarcastic way of looking at the world. Maybe it's part of some built-in defense mechanism, an armor we build up to protect ourselves from the stupid stuff. Maybe it's just us being goofy. Whatever it is, I love it. It's a huge part of what this book is all about, because it's a huge part of who I am.

If you've ever worked in a bar or restaurant, I'm fairly positive you'll get it. If you haven't, I can only hope.

Either way, take it in the spirit it was intended.

More than anything, I hope you get at least half the fun out of it as I had writing it.

C.J. Spaulding

May 2016

CHAPTER ONE
DOES NOT PLAY WELL ITH OTHER CHILDREN

It's a Saturday evening in July about eight years ago, give or take. I'm working a busy happy hour in Myrtle Beach, South Carolina. If I had to guess, I'd say it's 120 degrees with 80 percent humidity.

I'm sweating like a Kardashian during an S.A.T. exam. My underpants are a balled up wad of mush, squishing between my legs with every step I take, and I've already decided to throw them away after my shift.

At this point in my service industry career, I'm working at a popular brewery and steakhouse. It's my fourth bar or restaurant in almost fifteen years, which is actually far below the industry standard for jumping around in this business. (By the following year, I'll be on my fifth.)

They call me a bartender, but as the bartenders are also responsible for all the tables in the bar as well as the twelve tables in the outdoor beer garden, I'm basically a server who makes my own drinks. I'm one of the veteran bartenders of the establishment.

This one is a brutal shift. There are two of us working the outside tables, six packed picnic tables each, and I don't think you could fit another person out here if you greased him down with lard and shot him into the crowd with a catapult.

One of my tables just got up and, even though it's dirty, cluttered with empty glasses, and the last few plates I haven't bussed yet, the Table Vultures are already on it, practically plowing through the people finishing up. They're like rabid dogs who haven't eaten in a week, planting themselves down in front of the last group's leftovers, staking their claim on the piece of real estate they will rule over for the next hour and a half. I'm surprised that no one urinates on the table to mark their territory.

I need to go bus and greet my new ten-top, but I can't. At the moment, I'm being held up by a large man wearing a Rebel flag tank top and a hat that says, "I Love Beer." For the past six minutes, he's been trying to decide between french fries and garlic mashed potatoes with his burger. The way he's agonizing over the decision, you'd think lives hang in the balance.

For those same six minutes, I've been thinking of out-of-the-way places I could hide his body.

Big Boy lets out a deep breath and says, "Maybe I should get the chips."

I want to claw his eyes out.

Instead, I reply, "The chips are very good. They're homemade Kettle chips with sea salt."

"I don't know," he sighs. "I'm not crazy about sea salt."

This guy is killing me.

I can feel the glares from my new table burning holes in the back of my neck. They're already complaining between themselves because nobody has greeted them in the twelve seconds since they sat down and because the table is filthy.

With my peripheral vision, I spot two empty beer glasses on table four. At table five, people have begun stacking their empty plates, expecting me to swing by and pick them up. The lady at table six, the one I suspect is downing ramekins of ranch dressing like they're shots of vodka, is looking around, trying to find me. She needs another fix, and from the look on her face, she needs it right now. The guy at table eight has his wallet out. He's ready to pay his check.

I'd love nothing more than to get over there and help these people, but I can't. Right now I'm stuck waiting for this knucklehead to decide on a carb. With every second he takes to make this life-altering decision, I fall deeper and deeper into a hole that will take longer and longer to dig myself out of. This guy, single-handedly, is putting me in the weeds.

When he starts talking again, I no longer hear what he's saying. He sounds like the teacher in the Charlie Brown cartoons.

"Womp womp womp womp."

All I can hear is my own voice, inside my head.

What in the hell am I doing here? How did it come to this? I'm a bright guy, reasonably intelligent, with above average social skills. Sure, I've made some questionable decisions in life, but is this really what I deserve? What on God's green earth made me think it was a good idea to become a bartender?

One bourbon. One scotch. One beer.

We've all heard the old blues song. It's a catchy little ditty, but as a drink order, it downright sucks.

I mean, what kind of bourbon do you want? House, rail or premium? How about one of those small batch bourbons that are so popular these days? How do you want it? Neat, on the rocks or with a mixer?

What about that scotch? Do you want the cheap stuff or something good? Were you looking for a single-malt or a blend? Did you want the 12-, 18-, or 20-year-old?

And that beer chaser you mentioned, did you want a draught, can, or bottle? Domestic or import? Do you want something light or one of those high-gravity beers?

Come on, buddy. Give me a little help here.

Welcome to my world.

They say that it takes a woman fifteen seconds to decide if she's going to sleep with a man when she meets him. I can guarantee it takes your bartender much less time to decide if he or she likes you. Five seconds, tops.

After about five more seconds, your bartender has you pegged. He knows whether you are rich or poor, married or single, a pompous ass or the salt of the Earth. Most importantly, he has decided what kind of tipper you are. He has you completely figured out before you've even placed your drink order.

If he or she is any good at tending bar, you will be none the wiser

How accurate are these astute presumptions? I would say there is a fifty/fifty chance these assumptions are entirely inaccurate, but what does that matter? That's why they're called *preconceived* notions.

It is widely believed that people who enter the restaurant business do it because they love being around other people. This may be true in some cases, but I don't believe I've ever met any of those cases. All the bartenders I know hate people.

That people-loving thing is just something we say in job interviews.

All right, hate might be a little strong. It's more like all of the bartenders I know have a very strong dislike for a large portion of the people they come into contact with. We genuinely like a few of them.

It's not that bartenders are inherently bad people. In fact, some of them are quite nice. It's just that they have been dealing with the bottom of the gene pool for the entire night for umpteen nights in a row and when you complain because there are ice particles in your chilled shot, it's hard not to automatically assume you're a jerk. It's nothing personal. It comes with the territory.

I've been a bartender, on and off, for more than twenty years. I've worked in neighborhood dives, high-volume chain restaurants, and one particularly high-end hotel bar.

When I began writing this, I was working at a busy tourist destination that averaged around $30,000 a night during the summer months. It was crazy busy and it probably jaded my view on things. Having your ass handed to you on a daily basis will do that.

These days, I work at a Four Diamond hotel bar, a pretty sweet gig in comparison, so I know a thing or two about the business.

If you have never had a job where you've dealt with the public, you are going to have a hard time grasping some of the concepts I'm going to lay on you.

Here's the first one.

People suck.

They're kind of like cattle, only not as smart.

Okay, maybe not all people, but certainly enough to screw up your Saturday night.

Don't get me wrong. Some of my best friends are people. In fact, there are millions of wonderful people roaming the Earth. Sometimes, a few of them stop by my bar.

I'm a bartender. That means I make my living fetching things for other people. Most of the time they have no idea what it is they want me to fetch. As well as being a professional fetcher, my job also requires me to be a TV Guide, a weather forecaster, and an all-around problem solver.

People tend to resemble all the different species of the animal world. Your average bar or restaurant is a virtual wild kingdom. As a bartender or server, you are stranded in the wilderness, surrounded by the wild animals. It can be a lot like that "Man vs. Wild" show. The one where the guy is out in the woods, all alone, fighting for survival, eating tree bark and drinking his own urine.

*On a side note, what is the big deal with drinking your own urine, anyway? I know people who do that when they run out of Dr. Pepper.

The true character of an animal always comes out at feeding time. Lions are basically big lazy house cats most of the time, but when they get hungry, the whole "king of the jungle thing" comes out.

Some animals are ferocious and come right at you, while others are sly and cunning, preferring to sneak up and pounce on you when you aren't looking. Others are timid and scavenger-like, and they prey on the kills of others, running out and snagging their meal before scampering back to the safety of the tree line. My guess is most animals lean toward the scavenger type.

People are the same way. Trust me, you see all the animal types in the restaurant business. When it's feeding time in the human world, the human animals can't help but show their true character. It's Mother Nature. It's just the way it is.

I have approached a table of elderly, respectable-looking people and asked if I could help them, only to get the deer in the headlights look in return. Wide-eyed and confused, their heads dart back and forth as they try to figure out what it is they should say or do.

You would think I'd challenged them to a duel.

These are the people you want to pat on the head and say, "It's going to be okay. I know ordering dinner can be scary and traumatic, but I'm going to help you through this. Everything is going to be all right."

I bet if I had scratched their bellies, their legs would start kicking back and forth.

These people are not the hunters. They are most definitely the gatherers. With these types of people, you have to talk softly and avoid sudden movements so you don't scare them off.

In other cases, the very same question can turn people into vicious predators.

"We want to EAT!" they'll snarl back at you.

Yeah, I kinda figured that might be why you came to a restaurant.

These people are the carnivores, and they want to make sure you know it, right from the start. They are the top of the food chain and they're going to eat no matter what, so it's best to just throw some raw meat in the center of the table and keep your distance.

I love the people who start rattling off everything they want from the second you approach. Drinks, appetizers, salad, soup…

It's like they've never been to a restaurant before and they're afraid you're going to run out of *everything*. These people remind me of dogs that try to eat all of the food before you take the bowl away. Even though you *never* take the bowl away.

I've seen people approach the hostess stand and give their drink and dinner order to the 16-year-old hostess before they're even seated.

Do you not understand how this works?

Isn't that like getting undressed in your doctor's waiting room and showing the receptionist the boil you want to have lanced? It might make you feel better, but in the long run it's not going to do you a lot of good.

People are funny. Well, funny or downright annoying, depending on who you talk to. I actually like people. Sometimes. Sometimes, I even like my job.

I'm always amazed when I see any kind of disaster on television and by the way people can pull together and step up when things get crazy. It's incredible to see the kinds of things ordinary people can accomplish when they have to. It renews my sense of hope and pride in the human spirit.

It's even more incredible when you consider these are the same people bitching at me because their hot wings are too hot.

Do you think I'm being too hard on people? Maybe you're one of those kindhearted souls who sees the good in everyone they meet. You've obviously never worked in a restaurant.

If you are one of those people, I can only suggest you go back to the TV news I mentioned. Aside from those natural disasters, look at all the other depressing things going on in the world. In every case, in every horrible situation, every messed up thing in the world, there is always some person behind it. People are always the ones screwing things up.

These are the same people who come into my bar and kill my good mood. This is usually the result of their rudeness, stupidity, and/or selfishness. While you're at it, you can throw in the truly weird, the socially awkward, and the disturbingly outgoing types.

Rule number one. If you take one thing from reading this, let it be that there is a difference between a *server* and a *servant*. Some people don't get that.

Here's a recent example. I'm working at the hotel bar one night and this lady orders a chicken Caesar salad. When it arrived, she complained because the salad leaves were not cut up small enough and she sent it back so the cooks could cut her lettuce into smaller pieces.

Let me repeat that.

She sent it back so the cooks could cut up her *lettuce* into smaller pieces.

When she complained, she did so like it was my fault, and like the knife and fork in front of her were insufficient tools to remedy this horrific problem.

Maybe I could chew it up for you and feed it to you like you were a baby bird.

Who does that? Are you really so high and mighty that cutting your own salad is beneath you? Do you actually need to relegate the *lowly* restaurant staff to the unseemly chore of chopping your greens down to dainty, bite-sized morsels so your hands are not soiled by such a vulgar act?

Unfortunately, she is not the only one who has made a demand like this. She is one of many, the high-maintenance hordes of rude and inconsiderate patrons who walk into bars and restaurants every day.

Thank goodness they aren't all like that.

I've been working in the restaurant business for most of my adult life. I could break it down into actual years, but I've been lying about it for so long I'm afraid you might blow it for me if I told you my actual age. If you've never seen me before, let's go with 35. If you have seen me before, let's go with 39. I've always liked that number.

People end up in the service industry for all sorts of reasons. Rarely is it inflicted as part of any penal sentence. In almost all cases, it is entirely voluntary.

This is the part where you decide if you like me or not. I know I've talked a lot of trash to this point, but I'm not half as bad as you think I am. If you were to come to my bar, you would have no idea I was anywhere near as big a jerk as I actually am. My customers generally love me. In fact, most of the time, I'm so nice I make myself want to vomit.

So, what does that say about me? Am I a fake? Am I full of shit?

Of course I am. That's my job, and I'm damn good at it.

If you were to come into my work place, you would have no idea how bad a mood I happened to be in that particular day, or how much I didn't want to be there. I'm always courteous and polite and I fetch you whatever you need. That's what I do.

By now, you are now probably wondering, "What in the hell this guy is doing here? What is this book really about? Where is this guy going with this thing?"

I've always wanted to write one of those insightful travel adventures. You know the kind. One of those books where the writer takes you along as he searches out the answers to some underlying question, like Tony Horwitz looking for the remnants of the Civil War in *Confederates in the Attic* or Chuck Klosterman trying to find out why it's a good career move for a rock star to die young in *Killing Yourself to Live.* Like Hunter S. Thompson searching for the American dream in *Fear and Loathing in Las Vegas* and like John Steinbeck roaming the country with his dog and trying to reacquaint himself with the people he was writing about in *Travels with Charlie.*

It's one of my favorite writing genres and I've always wanted to take a crack at it. The major obstacle for me is, I have no major question to answer and I have nowhere in particular to go. I couldn't afford to take the time off work if I did.

Somehow, this is what I've come up with. A travel adventure story with no travel and very little adventure, trying to answer a question I haven't even come up with yet.

I will try to present a fair and insightful look at my profession, and I promise you, when it comes down to either giving you a clear and comprehensive look at the industry or going for the cheap laugh, I will almost always go with the latter.

Up until this point in my writing career I've only attempted fiction, so this should be interesting. Well, interesting or completely boring. You be the judge.

The thing I love (and hate) about writing is that it's kind of like bobbing for apples in an ocean of your own limitations. The only thing you can do is just get out there and start going at it, waiting to see what you come up with.

As I mentioned earlier, I worked at a very popular bar in a resort town. It was a microbrewery which happened to boast one of the best and busiest happy hours in all of Myrtle Beach. After my writing career tanks and I am left penniless and living on the streets, I will most likely still need to earn an income so I have decided not to use the real name of the place in my story, just in case I go back looking for a job. I will call it the Freedom Steakhouse and Brewery.

I realize there is a good chance you may be able to use the information I've provided to figure out where it is I worked (especially since there are only two breweries in MB). My lawyers assure me that as long as I don't use the company's real name I can not be sued or denied employment for writing this.

Who am I kidding? I don't have a lawyer, but I do know a few and I am convinced that if I were to ask them they would tell me something along those lines.

I worked at the Freedom Steakhouse and Brewery for close to seven years. In dog years, that would be 42 years. In bug years, that would be somewhere in the vicinity of 9,000 years. Actually, I don't know if there is any such thing as bug years, but if there were, I am pretty sure those calculations are accurate.

The thing about tending bar is it's kind of like babysitting a pack of wolves. When things are going well it's usually pretty good, but when things turn, they tend to get ugly quick.. Not to mention, if they smell fear on you, you're totally screwed.

I've heard people say that a monkey could do my job. This is total myth and complete fabrication. Most species of monkey could not even see over the bar, much less reach the bottles and hanging glasses. You could argue they could climb up and get what they needed, but most of the bars I have ever worked in frown upon employees climbing around the bar back and swinging from the rafters.

I will concede there are some very bright monkey types out there and there might even be some that could remember more drink recipes than me, but this in no way makes them more qualified to tend bar.

With their ambidextrous feet and hands, you could also argue that they could carry more than I do, but when you figure in the cost of spilled drinks and the importance of communication skills, I could out-bartend any monkey on the planet. I'm not even going to bring up the health code issues that said monkey would bring to the table.

That said, they are really cute and people do love monkeys…

I bet a monkey would clean up in tips.

You are probably wondering how I ended up in the bar business. Either that or you have already tossed this book aside and gone on to something more interesting. I am going to assume, for the sake of argument, you are still reading. It makes the process of writing this seem more pertinent.

I got into this business when I was in my early twenties. After four years in the Army, I was bumming around Baltimore and trying to figure out what I was going to do (something I am actually still doing). I knew I was going to end up going back to school, eventually, and I needed something to keep busy and make some money.

My aunt worked at a little bar on the outskirts of the city called O'Brady's Saloon. I will go ahead and give you the real name because I am pretty sure I'm not going to say anything that could get me sued and I'm reasonably positive that I won't be back there looking for work anytime soon.

I started hanging out there a lot. Hence, it became what I like to refer to as my hangout. One day it dawned on me that since I was there anyway, I should get a job there. I took my brilliant idea to the woman who was kind of running the place for her ex-husband and she agreed.

"Be here tomorrow at four," I think she said.

That's how I got started in the bar business. The next day I followed her around the bar and she showed me where everything was, how to use the cash register, and some of the basic drink recipes. I think I was working by myself the following day.

I never had to take one of those bartending classes or anything. I just kind of picked it up as I went.

Speaking of bartending classes, I need to stop and talk about them for a second. Not only have I never taken one, but I'm not sure I actually know anyone who has.

Let me rephrase that. I'm not sure I know of anyone who has taken bartending classes who actually works as a bartender. I've met people who have taken those classes and were interested in getting a bartending job but I'm not sure I've ever known one to actually do it.

My guess is the kind of people who take classes on how to bartend are usually the kind of people who should never be allowed behind an actual bar. They are probably much better at taking classes than at fetching stuff. I could be wrong on this point and, I have to confess, it's not something I feel too strongly about one way or the other, but I have a hunch I'm at least partially correct.

If you are reading this and you are a graduate of one of these fine institutions, who has gone on to be a successful bartender in your own right, please do not send me hate mail.

I have actually talked to other bartenders who have expressed an interest in attending these classes. These are people who are already in the industry and want to brush up on their bartending skills and pick up on the latest trends and techniques.

These people are idiots.

Once again, if you are a bartender who has been working in the field and has gone back to take a bartending class, please do not send me hate mail. I get enough from my family.

I just don't understand why anyone would want to pay money to learn something they already know so they can do something they're already doing. I could be wrong on this one too, but I just don't get it. Could you even imagine sitting around and listening to some bozo drone on about how to make a gin and tonic?

As far as the whole trends and techniques thing goes, basically we put drinks in glasses. I'm guessing that we don't do it a whole lot differently than bartenders did it in the 1700s.

Sure, some things have changed. We have things like refrigeration, ice, beer nuts, and the Red-Headed Slut, but basically the premise is the same. Your customer gives you money and you give them booze. It's not like we're doing open-heart surgery.

By the way, when I said Red-Headed Slut, I was referring to the shot, not that girl we all knew in college..

To get back to my point, don't get me wrong, either. I'm not saying it doesn't require a certain set of skills to do what I do. I've already made a mildly convincing argument against monkeys being able to pull it off. It's just that I don't think any of the skills required for bartending can be taught in a school. They have nothing to do with making drinks. The hardest part of what I do is all about dealing with people, and you can either do that or you can't.

There's another thing worth mentioning about tending bar. It's another perk that comes with the job. When I go to work, I am constantly surrounded by beautiful, young girls. It comes with the territory.

Many of you are probably thinking, "That must suck."

I can assure you, it does not.

Pretty much everywhere I've ever worked, I have been surrounded by a bevy of young lovelies, some of them servers, others fellow bartenders. It's a business where attractive women can make a good deal of money, and they tend to flock to it.

Just look at the place where I'm currently employed. I keep referring to it as the hotel bar, but that sounds so impersonal. I suppose I should come up with a fake name for it.

The hotel is one of the largest, most successful chains in the world. I can only imagine the kind of legal team they have lurking in the wings, waiting to pick my bones clean. Forget about getting fired or sued, they have the power to make me disappear completely.

"What ever happened to that guy who was working on the book about bars?"

"What guy? Never heard of him."

To be on the safe side, from here on out, I will refer to the hotel bar as the Big Digs Hotel Bar. That should do the trick.

At the Big Digs, we have a staff of four bartenders and usually five or six cocktail servers, depending on the time of year. On an average night, we might run one bartender and two servers. These cocktail servers are responsible for the tables throughout the bar area, and their jobs entail much more than just serving cocktails. In fact, people tend to like our bar more than the hotel's actual restaurant, so it's not uncommon for us to do two or three as many dinners as them.

Our cocktail servers might be part of the reason, as well. They wear little black cocktail dresses. Again, this does not suck.

All of the girls I work with are drop-dead gorgeous, and they are also incredibly hard workers and very good at what they do. When our bar gets hit, it gets hit hard, and you have to be on your game to keep up with the onslaught. Over the years, I've seen plenty of pretty faces who couldn't quite hack it and they are usually weeded out pretty quick, no matter what they look like.

I'm considerably older than most of the girls who make their way through the Big Digs, so it's not like there is any hanky-panky going on. Just the same, I don't mind being surrounded by the eye candy.

Over the years, I have become good friends with most of them and a few are among the all-time favorites I've ever worked with.

I like to affectionately refer to the girls at the Big Digs as my She Devils in Black Dresses. When I'm working service bar (making drinks for their tables), they constantly bark orders and yell at me, bossing me around and making outrageous demands of me. It's a lot like working with my ex-wife.

One Halloween, they all got together and came to work with pitchforks and wearing horns. Somewhere, I have a great picture of me, surrounded by my She Devils in Black Dresses. I will treasure it always.

All this talk of pretty girls has me thinking about another side to the business. Many of you might think working in a bar is all wild parties, beautiful women, and crazy sex. (What, did you think there wasn't going to be any sex in this book? It would be a pretty lame book if it didn't have any sex.)

I hate to disappoint you, but it is not like that at all. Don't get me wrong, it has its moments.

These days, I'm settled down with my significant other, doing my thing and staying out of trouble. But it wasn't always like this.

In my early years as a bartender, there were times when my profession presented certain opportunities I might not have had if I had been working as an accountant. Let's face it – bars are a great place to meet women. When you are the most sober person in the room and the pseudo ringleader of the party, it does not hurt your chances of getting lucky. The sheer number of people you meet in a bar on a nightly basis increases your odds substantially.

I was a young man, an ex-paratrooper after four years in the service, and it was the late '80s. There was a part of me that felt like I'd missed out on a lot of things while in the Army, and I saw bartending as a way of making up for lost time.

I did some things back then I wouldn't want to see my kids do, if you know what I mean. What the hell, right?

All of this is leading up to one of my favorite O'Brady's stories. O'Brady's had a kitchen and was a popular place to get blue crabs. Past the bar, some steps led down to a dining room filled with picnic tables. These tables were covered with brown paper. Anyone who has ever eaten blue crabs knows what this is all about.

After I'd been working there for a while, one morning around three o'clock the bar is closed, and I'm having sex on top of one of these picnic tables with this beautiful blonde biker chick. Her name was something like Lacey and I remember she wore tight jeans and a leather vest. How cool is that?

Hey, I was young, and, like I said, it was the '80s. Don't judge.

Anyhow, the clean-up man lived upstairs from the bar, but he rarely came down before four or five in the morning. This night he decided to get an early start, and he walked in on Lacey and me doing the dirty.

I think I said something like, "John, I'm kind of busy right now. Come back later."

He did.

The next night, I was nervous about going into work. I was sure John was going to tell the owner what he'd seen me doing, and I had no idea how my boss would react.

Sure enough, John had spilled the beans and I called aside. He was not very happy with me and I will never forget what he said.

"CJ," he said. "Rule number one in this business is don't get crabs on the crabs."

True story.

I am actually reconsidering using the bar's real name now.

Ah, those good ol' O'Brady's days, when life was fresh, the days were long, and I spent a good deal of my time thinking with the wrong part of my anatomy. Oh, well.

It's hard to believe all these years since the O'Brady's days that I'm still out here doing it. I never intended for it to be a career. I still don't. It was just some gig I thought might be fun for a while.

Most of the people I know in this industry have similar stories. We all got into it to make some quick and easy money. The thing we all found out after the fact was the money isn't always quick and it's seldom easy. (Refer back up to that wad of sweaty underpants I mentioned earlier.)

There are certainly harder ways to earn a living, and I can't complain about the money. Most people would probably be surprised by how much the average bartender actually makes. I can make as much in a night as some people make in a week. For the most part, these people are panhandlers, crackheads, and people with mental handicaps that prevent them from working real jobs, but still.

By the way, if you work for the IRS, everything I just said was a lie.

While the money can be great at times, it can also be extremely inconsistent. It's not uncommon during the slow times for bartenders and servers to consider selling things like blood, plasma, and vital organs just to pay the rent. Or for beer money.

Many bartenders and servers work more than one job. I know a lot of people who do something else besides tend bar. Some work in restaurants part time and others are working until they can get started in their chosen field. (I'm actually a writer and photographer.)

In every one of these cases, no matter how long they have been tending bar, or how many hours they log behind the bar, or when they finally get rolling in whatever profession they are working toward, they always (100 percent of the time) refer to the other job as their *real job.*

"I can't work on Thursday because I'm working my real job."

"It's time I went out and got a real job."

We all do it, and I guess it says a lot about the way we perceive what we do. Maybe I just found the underlying question I will spend this book trying to answer.

Something else I need to mention is the lifestyle that goes along with working in the service industry. In all my years in the business, I've known very few people who didn't partake in the lifestyle to some degree. Every server in every town knows where the best places are to eat and drink. This is because it is a huge part of the lifestyle.

The rest of the world merely passes through the restaurant industry. We live in it.

However, no matter what town or city you travel to, go up to your server or bartender and ask where the best bars and restaurants are. At first, they will probably lie to you and tell you the one they work at, and the one you are already in, is by far the coolest, most happening, and finest-eatingist place ever invented.

They are trained to say this.

When you ask the question, their brain automatically shuts off and the words are triggered by a chemical reaction. They can't help it.

I have actually come out of a smoky, trance-like state and heard myself muttering in a monotone voice, "Freedom Steakhouse and Brewery has the finest food in Myrtle Beach."

I believe the restaurant management staff puts something in our food that causes this to happen, but I have no proof of this.

One day, standing by our hostess stand, a tourist couple poked their heads in the front door and asked our 16-year-old hostess where they could get a good steak. She sent them to a place three doors down.

After they had gone, I asked her if she realized that, not only did we serve steaks, but the word *steakhouse* was actually a part of our name. She told me that she didn't realize the people were asking about us.

Come to think of it, I never saw that 16-year-old girl eat at our restaurant, so maybe she wasn't affected by whatever it is they put in our food. Any of the rest of us probably would have said, in a monotone voice, "Freedom Steakhouse and Brewery has the finest food in Myrtle Beach."

While the average family might eat out to dinner once every two weeks (I have no idea how accurate this is and I'm too lazy to look it up), the average restaurant worker probably only eats once every two weeks. (This is not always the case and I may be exaggerating a tad, as I'm much more interested in making my point than in any sort of factual content this book may or may not have. True, if said restaurant worker is married or has children there is a much more likelihood that they will eat at home more often.) Even if this were the case, I would stake everything I own on the fact that restaurant people are in bars and restaurants at least ten times as often as regular people (on average). Now, before you bar and restaurant junkies start getting all excited, I should warn you that my ex-wife got most of my stuff, so I don't really own all that much.

I know people who eat in restaurants every day of their lives. Sometimes two or three times a day. If I actually ate three times a day, I would probably be one of them.

And we haven't even started talking about drinking yet.

People in this business like to consume alcohol.

It would be easy to dismiss all of us as raging alcoholics. But I don't think that it's as simple as that. There is much more to it.

I feel like I need to stop here and say a few words about drinking. I am not promoting the abuse of alcohol. I do not want to get hate mail from M.A.D.D. or from anyone out there with alcohol issues. Alcohol is a part of all of our lives and I'm just commenting on it. If you don't believe me, stop by your local watering hole between the hours of 4 and 7 p.m. The drinking of alcohol is a large part of our culture. Good or bad, it is a part of who we are, and it's not just part of American culture, either.

Assuming that we are all adults here, I believe that you can do anything you want until you infringe on the rights of other people. That doesn't mean that we can all get loaded and get behind the wheel of a car. We can't. If we have learned nothing else from watching sporting events on TV, it is that we should all drink responsibly.

There is also a dark side to this part of the lifestyle and, if you aren't careful, it can turn around and bite you in the ass. I've seen it happen many times, but that's another topic for future chapters.

You would think that after working in a bar or restaurant for five days straight, the last place a person in this business would want to spend their day off would be a bar or restaurant. This is not even close to the case. It is actually the first place most of them want to be.

I have heard people say that after waiting on people all week, they just want to be waited on, too. I believe this to be partially true but I think it's much deeper than that. I think it goes back to what draws us into this business. It's a part of our makeup, how were built. It's in our blood, somehow.

Earlier, I mentioned that the money is good in this racket, but what I failed to mention is that the lifestyle that we lead demands that we spend more money. We don't need Martha Stewart to tell us that it's cheaper to eat and drink at home. You can save more money by going home with a six-pack than you can by drinking in a bar. So why are we in the business compelled to spend our off time in another bar or restaurant?

The same thing that drew us to the industry in the first place.

After a particularly hard night, most people in this business love nothing more than to sit around and talk about how particularly hard our night was. Usually, we do this over a cocktail.

If it was a particularly slow night, you might find us all sitting around discussing how particularly slow our night was. Usually, we do this over a cocktail.

Good, bad, great, hard, slow. It doesn't matter. We do it over a cocktail.

It's a part of the process, part of what brought us into this crazy game, and part of what keeps us here. It's the best part of what I do, after a busy night, sitting around with the people who become more like family than friends or coworkers, sharing our common experiences and laughing about the silly, stupid things that happened to us or complaining about things when times are bad.

I suppose the alcohol is a part of it, but it isn't the biggest part. It's a residual of what we do, a perk of the business. It's a bond we share and the after-work cocktail is how we choose to celebrate it.

I've always thought camaraderie was kind of a stupid word. When I think of it, I think of two guys in the French Foreign Legion. (I'm not sure what that means, either, but I can't think of a better word to use.)

Working a crazy night in summer when the you-know-what hits the fan is a lot like being in a gang fight and the people you work alongside become like members of your posse. You spend more time with these people than you do with your family.

I have a friend (Kira) I used to work with, who, when we are all hanging out after work, liked to say, "I love us."

There is a certain feeling of belonging to some sort of club that comes with this job. A sense of being included in on something that others aren't. It's a sense of being where the action is.

But where exactly is the action? It is, of course, where the people are. The bars and restaurants.

Those of us in this business all pretty much hate not being where the action is. We can't stand the thought of missing out on something. This is why we are drawn back to the bars and restaurants on our days off, and this is what initially draws us into this business in the first place.

We love to talk about how much we hate people.

"People suck."

"I hate people."

I am guilty of this myself. I say it all the time. In my defense, I think it is a funny sentiment and I will probably never stop saying it.

The thing is, we really don't hate people. The reason we are all in this stupid business and not out there working real jobs is because we really do love people. It's that craving to be surrounded by people that brought us here to begin with, and it's that craving to be around people that keeps us here, putting up with all the craziness we are forced to endure. It's addictive, and if you do it long enough, it's hard to imagine yourself sitting in front of a computer, in some cubicle, void of human contact.

In the long run, I guess we actually do play well with other children, after all.

I realize this totally contradicts everything I said in the beginning of this chapter, but life itself is a giant contradiction. Why should my book be any different?

As far as me hating on people and poking fun at them, I doubt if I will ever stop doing that, and you can look forward to much more of it in the upcoming chapters, but I will admit, I'm certainly not perfect. One of my biggest flaws is I don't always know when to not cross the line. Sometimes I forget about the line entirely.

Not long after I'd started working at Big Digs, one slow afternoon my only customer was a sweet, elderly woman. We were sitting there chatting, watching CNN, and I thought we'd built up a nice little repartee.

On the news, a story came on about some guy in the Midwest who had been arrested for something or the other, and, when they searched his home, they found a large freezer filled with the bodies of dead cats. Apparently, he'd been going around his neighborhood, killing these poor cats and sticking them in his freezer. There were hundreds of them.

When she saw the story, the woman at my bar gasped in shock and said, "That's horrible!"

"Yes," I agreed. "That is horrible. Everybody knows you can't freeze cat. You have to eat that fresh."

So, what have we learned so far?

1. The restaurant business is chock-full of a bunch of hard-drinking, people-loving, people haters who got into it for the quick, easy money that isn't actually quick or easy.

2. You can't freeze cat.

Confused? That's okay. As long as you don't get crabs on the crabs, everything will be fine.

CHAPTER TWO

IF YOU DON'T EAT YOUR MEAT
YOU CAN'T HAVE ANY PUDDING

H ow can you have any pudding if you don't eat your meat? Talk about your age-old question. Pink Floyd really pegged it with that one.

The thing is, it's totally true. People really do want their pudding, and they want it right now. I think this speaks of a behavioral pattern in people. Maybe it speaks more about the times we live in. All I know is, somebody better be getting some pudding soon or the you-know-what is going to hit the fan.

And guess whose job it is to fetch the pudding?

Let me tell you, when people want their pudding, they are not shy about asking for it. In fact, they can be outright jerks about it.

We can all be jerks when we want to, can't we?

This brings up another question.

Why are all of us such jerks?

I am not saying that every single person is a jerk. Mother Theresa seemed like she was pretty cool and that Pope John Paul guy seemed like he was all right, but most of the rest of us fall into the jerk category. How's that for a broad statement?

We are all a bunch of self-centered egomaniacs who are pretty much concerned about one thing. Ourselves. It's just that some of us are better at hiding it then others.

I personally believe that I am the coolest person on the entire planet. I also fully understand that my guidelines for cool are completely different than those of any other person on the planet. This, I believe, is perfectly normal. It's human nature.

I know what you're thinking. *Not me. I'm not like that. I am a very nice person with a lot of friends and I go out of my way to do nice things for other people.*

Whatever.

This is not something I see as a particularly bad thing about our species. It is what it is. We are all preoccupied with ourselves and with getting whatever it is that we want for ourselves. We are consumers.

We consume. It's what we do. We consume everything we can get our hands on and, along the way, we leave a path of destruction and garbage. If you don't believe me, ask planet Earth what she thinks of us as a people. I'm pretty certain she would agree with me on this one.

That said, I will agree that even if we are all indeed jerks, we are all jerks on different levels of jerkiness. This is where our social skills (or lack thereof) come into play.

We all want what we want, but we all have different ways of going about getting what we want. Most of us are adept at using various degrees of pleasantry and politeness to achieve our goals of self-indulgence. Others, not so much. These are the people who I always seem to find myself waiting on.

Earlier, I mentioned that I work in a resort town. A large percentage of the people I come in contact with during the summer months are on vacation. It never ceases to amaze me how many of these vacationers are in incredibly bad moods.

You would think that it would all be happy smiles and positive attitudes. After all, you're on vacation. Fun in the sun. No work for the next week or two. Paradise. Right?

Wrong.

It is not at all like that. Vacationers are, for the most part, rude and impatient people with little or no regard for anyone around them. They act more like refugees stranded in a foreign land than people spending their hard-earned money on some relaxing fun.

This is especially true of men (husbands and fathers). I can only guess this is brought on from being cooped up with their wives and children for days on end with no break. Dad would rather be off playing golf or watching strippers. I understand that. What I don't get is why they feel the need to take it out on *me*.

Another friend of mine came up with a theory on this that's quite interesting. She believes a large portion of the people we wait on are on their one vacation getaway, after serving their time in whatever cubicle or office they work in, and after taking an entire year of shit off of whomever it is they take shit off of, when they walk through our door, it's their turn to dish out the very thing they have been getting for the last twelve months. For two weeks a year, they are in charge and they're going to make sure everyone knows it.

It's sad to think that people could be so shallow and petty, but if

I have learned nothing else from working in this business, it's that people are shallow and petty. I believe my friend's theory to be at least partially true, but then I believe that pretty much everything is grounded in truth. Either way it's pretty funny.

Whatever the reason behind it, people are just plain rude at times.

If your server or bartender comes up to you and the first words out of your mouth are, "Get me a beer," I have something to say to you.

YOU ARE A JERK!

Plain and simple.

I realize there are a lot of people out there who aren't as restaurant-savvy as those of us in the business, so let me give you a few pointers here.

Here are some sure tell signs that your bartender or server hates your guts. These are things to avoid doing if you don't want the last person touching your food to think that you are the scum of the earth.

If you bang your empty glass on the bar when you are ready for another drink, there is a very good chance your server wishes you dead.

If you whistle at your server or call him or her over in the same manner you would a dog, I can guarantee your server is secretly trying to cast some sort of voodoo spell on you and your family.

If your server is in the middle of taking an order at the table next to yours and you grab hold of his or her arm or scream because you need an extra side of ranch dressing, your server would like nothing better than to see your head on a stick.

If every time your server comes to your table you ask for one more little thing, your server is fantasizing about torturing you to death. We realize that our job is to fetch stuff for you, but if you keep asking me to fetch one little thing every time I come up, it doesn't leave much time for me to fetch all the other stuff that my other tables want me to fetch for them.

This is all simple stuff. It's common courtesy and it goes back to what I said in Chapter One about the difference between a server and a servant.

All of this directly relates to what I was saying about people wanting what they want and the various ways they go about getting it. I concede that paying customers have the right to get what they are paying for in a timely manner. You should expect quality product and excellent service, and if you don't get these things, you have been cheated.

At the same time, you also have a responsibility when interacting in the world around you. There are certain guidelines that we should all adhere to whenever we are out and about in public.

Your bartender or server is not one of the dregs of society. Actually, this may not always be the case, but it still isn't fair to automatically assume your bartender or server is a dreg of society. (I'm not even sure what a dreg actually is, but it doesn't sound very flattering.)

Sure, there are a lot of scumbags out there schlepping drinks and serving food, but not all of us are degenerates and lowlifes. My guess is the percentage of these types of people in our industry is not much different than the percentage found in the accounting or insurance fields. I would even wager the percentage is much lower than that found in used car sales. (Again, I have no actual data to back this up and I'm pretty much shooting from the hip here.)

The point is, people are people, and whether they are fetching you stuff or providing some other service, they deserve to be treated with a certain amount of respect. This seems like such a basic thing, but you would be surprised at how many people don't get that.

One night while I was working, a coworker of mine came up to me. She was incensed. She was waiting on a large group of people. A family.

While in the process of taking a dinner order from one of the women at the table, another woman began screaming at her because she wanted to order a rack of ribs. This was while her family member was trying to explain what it was *she* wanted for dinner.

"CAN YOU TAKE MY ORDER?" the woman yelled, interrupting the other.

How rude is that? She can't wait fifteen seconds for her server to get to her? Even 5-year-olds know how to wait their turn.

If you have never had a bunch of people trying to tell you eight different things at once, I can tell you from experience that it's not much fun. It can actually be very frustrating and all it does is back up the whole process.

This particular friend of mine actually handled it well. She turned to the rude woman and said, "Yes ma'am, I understand that you want to order ribs, but right now I'm in the middle of taking your sister's dinner order. I'll be with you in one second."

Of course, when she relayed the story to me she didn't use language anywhere near as polite as that. I won't tell you exactly what she said, but some of the words began with the letters M, F, and C. You do the math.

So, what is it that could make a normal person act this way?

I think most of it boils down to the fact that there are a lot of people out there who aren't very bright. That's putting it mildly. I've seen old tires that are brighter than some of the people I wait on (they have better personalities, too).

You can take some of my customers and put a crossword puzzle between them and a rock and the rock would have a better chance of finishing it.

If you don't believe me, just watch some of these people try to figure out what 15 percent of their dinner bill is. It's like they're doing calculus problems on the back of their dinner check.

Y+X-Z= the server is screwed.

If you ever want to see, first hand, how bad our education system is, watch some of these people try to figure out the correct tip. They might as well be trying to split the atom with a butter knife. I don't even get upset when people like this leave me a bad tip anymore. I just feel sorry for them. They honestly don't know any better.

If there comes a time when I can't figure out what 15 percent of 64 dollars is, please put a bullet in my head.

Here's a simple formula for anyone who really can't figure out how to come up with the proper tip amount.

Take your total bill and move the decimal point one to the left. You have now figured out 10 percent. Divide that in half and add the two together.

So, if your bill is $100.00,

Ten percent is $10.00.

Half of that is $5.00.

10 + 5 = $15.00.

How hard is that?

I won't even get into the fact that 18 percent is now the industry standard. I don't want anyone's head to explode.

Here's another one I see all the time.

If you and your friend both come to happy hour and you each get an order of chicken wings and a beer and the tab is $10.00, you should not need separate checks. If you do, you are both idiots. You should not have to be Albert Einstein to figure out this baffling mathematical equation.

If you can't figure out that you each owe $5.00, maybe you shouldn't be in a bar or restaurant. You might be better off in some kind of state-sanctioned home. It's probably better for everyone involved.

You might think I'm exaggerating. Either that or you are still back there trying to do the math problems I presented. Just in case, I will type slower so you can catch up.

How about this one?

If you ask me for your check and I go and get it, when I come back, don't just hand me your credit card. I mean, at least pretend to look at the check. You just made me go all the way over there and print it out. Humor me and act like you didn't just waste valuable minutes of my life that I will never get back.

At the very least, if you are just going to hand me a credit card anyway and not even glance at the check, then don't ask for the bill in the first place. Just give me the damned credit card.

Here's another.

"I hate to be a pain in the ass but…"

You have to love it when somebody starts off with that sentence. And by love it, I mean hate it.

You know what? Then just don't. I mean, you hate it and I certainly hate it so if you just don't do it we'll all be a lot happier.

Of course, I should probably point out that people who start off with this phrase are seldom ever a pain in the ass. This is not always the case, but I'd say eight out of ten times, they are not a pain at all. Okay, maybe six out of ten. Well, just to be on the safe side, let's say half the time.

One time, a guy asked me how big our pizzas were. I informed him that at the Freedom Steakhouse and Brewery we serve a ten-inch pie.

"How many slices is that?" he asked.

I told him we cut them into eight slices.

This was the next thing he said, while shaking his head. "I'm good for two or three slices, but there's no way I could eat eight."

I'm guessing he wasn't in town for the brain surgeon convention.

I could have offered to have the pizza cut into two or three slices, especially for him, but I didn't. I could have even tried to explain that, even if we cut the pizza into a million slices, it was still a ten-inch pie and would still be the exact same amount of food, but again, I didn't.

Instead, I stood there staring at him, wondering how he was able to function out in the real world without inflicting harm on himself and others. Obviously, he wasn't quite smart enough to eat pizza anyway.

Even at the Big Digs Hotel bar, I see it all the time.

A guy walked into my bar the other day and said, "I want vodka."

"Sure thing," told him. "How would you like that?"

He shrugged his shoulders and replied, "I don't know. How does it come?"

It comes in hermetically sealed test tubes and packed in dry ice. What do you mean, how does it come?

I understand there are some of us with more experience when it comes to drinking than others, but really? If you're ordering a vodka, how can you not know how to order a vodka? I would think, from television and movies alone, a person could figure out how to order a vodka and tonic.

One lady came in a while back and asked me how much vodka was. (Again with the vodka.) I explained that it depended on what kind of vodka she wanted and on how she wanted it served. After all, a vodka martini is more expensive than a regular drink or a shot of vodka.

After I gave her the price, she told me she just wanted a shot of regular vodka, so I poured a shot of our house vodka. For a few seconds, she stared at the shot with confusion.

"Don't I get any ice?" she finally asked.

Another time, a guy walked up, slapped his hand on the bar and said, "Whiskey!"

Do you want me to leave the bottle, like we're in an old Cowboy movie?

Where do these people come from?

When you walk into the Freedom Steakhouse and Brewery, there is a large glass window behind the bar that separates the barroom from the brewery. The brewery houses the large copper tanks where the beer is mixed, brewed, and fermented before being transferred to the serving tanks above. I'm guessing there is close to a million dollars in brewing equipment in there.

At least three times a day, people would ask me if it's where we made the homemade beer.

Nope, that's all for show. We actually make the beer in five-gallon buckets in the men's room.

Not to mention that I would be a rich man if I had a nickel for every time someone asked me what our Raspberry Wheat beer tasted like.

Bananas.

People just don't use their noggins.

To anyone who has never worked in the service industry, I know this must seem like I am making all this up. I wish I was.

The re is a part of me that feels like I'm telling a bunch of old bar jokes.

A guy walks into a bar with a parrot on his shoulder...

Unfortunately, not only has all this happened, but it occurs on a regular basis.

I suppose anyone who has a driver's license is used to dealing with the stupidity of others to some degree. For all I know, stories like these may be commonplace in every profession in America. I somehow doubt it.

At the same time, there are those golden moments, those magical instances where everything comes together, when the skies open and it's like it's raining salt-water taffy. It's like a gift from heaven.

Of course, I'm talking about when a total nimrod makes a complete jackass out of himself.

This one time, I had a guy sitting at my bar. He was a total dork, but he thought he was Mister Cool and a bag of chips. This guy was cocky, condescending, and just plain rude.

Some random girl ended up sitting next to him and he was doing his best to talk up his best game. What he was really doing was just being obnoxious.

He might have thought he had a chance, but he was doomed from the start. She was barely being polite to him.

(Your bartender can always tell when you are being shot down long before it ever occurs to you.)

He finally realized he wasn't getting anywhere with her and this made him even more of a jerk.

"Tab! Now!" he said to me, in possibly the rudest way you can ask for your check.

I printed it out and gave it to him, but he tossed it back at me with a huff.

"There's no place to sign and there is no place to write in the tip," he pointed out to me, like he was speaking to a 5-year-old.

This is when I got to explain to him that I had merely printed up a copy of his bill and he hadn't actually given me a credit card yet. I made sure to say it like I was talking to a 3-year-old.

The best part of the whole deal was the look that the girl was giving him.

Here's another one. It was a quiet night at the Big Digs and there are only a few people sitting at my bar. One of these people is an attractive woman in her mid- to late-thirties who is keeping to herself and enjoying an appetizer and a glass of wine. In walks an older gentleman in a conservative gray suit. I'd guess him in his late fifties. He orders an expensive scotch on the rocks and takes notice of the woman sitting alone.

Before you can say dirty old man, he is at her side and in her ear. He offers to buy her a drink or take her to dinner. She politely declines. The guy in the suit keeps at it, but is getting nowhere. After a while, he steps outside for a cigarette.

When he comes back, he has a renewed vigor. He's on a mission to pick up this woman. He offers to take her to the finest restaurant in town, to take her out for drinks and dancing. He's telling her how beautiful she is and how much he wants to get to know her. He's bragging about his car, his beach house, and his fat bank account. The entire time, the woman is respectfully turning him down and trying to blow him off as courteously as possible.

This goes on for twenty minutes. I'm not going to lie. It was difficult to watch. It was a little like seeing your grandmother try to do a keg stand.

The guy isn't wearing down. He's determined to convince this attractive lady to go out with him.

Eventually, another woman enters the bar. She storms right over to the guy and whips him around by the arm.

"Hey, dumbass," she says. "When you went outside to call me, you never hung up your phone. I've been listening to every word you were saying on the drive over here!"

You can't make this stuff up.

The guy reaches into his breast pocket and pulls out his phone, staring down at it in horror. After a thorough berating, the couple leaves, the woman steaming mad, the guy with his tail between his legs. My entire bar burst into laughter the moment they were gone.

It was one of those priceless moments, the kind that reminds you there is a greater force ruling the universe and the kind that makes you appreciate the little things in life. It was one of those darndest things I get to see from my vantage point behind the bar from time to time.

Before I came to the Freedom Steakhouse and Brewery, I worked at another place that is actually in the same complex. I can't think of anything particularly good to say about that place so I will go ahead and make up a fake name for that one, too. There is probably a greater likelihood that I could end up getting sued by them. We will call it the Crustacean House. It was a seafood restaurant that specialized in crabs. You figure it out.

I was working a busy summer night with another friend of mine. She was possibly the most sarcastic person I've ever worked with, and she didn't like to take crap from people at all.

At the Crustacean House, we didn't have much of a bar crowd

and it was mostly people waiting to be seated in the dining room. People waiting to eat are, for the most part, especially angry people. It's that whole feeding time in the jungle thing.

The wait was probably an hour or so, and this guy ordered a beer and an appetizer from my friend while he was waiting for his table. My friend turns around and punches his order into the computer (which was right across from this guy). When she is done, she grabs a silverware roll and sits it in front of him.

At this moment, the guy looks up at her and says, "Where's my appetizer?"

This friend of mine never had a lot of patience when it came to stupidity. She walked back over to the computer and said, "Let me explain how this process works. You order the food from me." She was speaking in a slow, exaggerated tone that a monkey could probably pick up on. Not the most subtle sarcasm I've ever witnessed.

"Then, I *punch* it in," she continued, turning toward the computer and pretending to retype his order.

"From there, it is transferred electronically through a series of wires to our *kitchen*. When the order prints out there, our cooks *cook* it, and when it's done they will bring it out to *you*."

The guy just sat there staring back at her in disbelief. It was a beautiful thing to witness.

Most of us don't say things like that to our customers. We just think them.

Whoever said the customer is always right never worked in any of the places I've worked. It's always been my experience that the customer rarely has any idea of what's actually going on.

Here are some more pointers.

If your bartender or server asks you how you are doing, he or she is not making a social call. They do not really care how your day was or how your Aunt Bertha is doing after the surgery. They want to know if you need anything. That is their job.

If you tell them everything is fine and then, when they are walking away from your table, you call them back to order a refill on your iced tea, do not expect to get a Christmas card from this person.

Here's one. If your bartender or server approaches you and asks if you would like something to drink, "I don't drink," is not a proper response.

How do you stay hydrated?

Technically, a drink does not have to contain alcohol to be considered a drink. Water, iced tea, Coca-Cola, or Sprite would all be correct answers to this question. If you answer your bartender or server in any other manner, you are simply backing up the entire system.

Rest assured, if you say anything stupid or rude to your server or bartender, everyone who works there knows about it in around 35 seconds. That is the average length of time it takes information to circulate through a restaurant staff. I can guarantee you that within two minutes of you saying it, there are other restaurant employees purposely walking by your table to see the *idiot* who said the stupid thing.

Who am I kidding? I love the stupid question. I live for the stupid question. It makes my entire day. The truth is, I love a good laugh as much as the next guy, and there is a part of me that lives for these moments. My motto in life is: *If you can't laugh at yourself, find someone else to laugh at. There are plenty to pick from.*

Some people say the only stupid question is the unasked question or there's no such thing as a stupid question. These people couldn't be any more incorrect. The stupid question is alive and well and I get asked it on an almost daily basis.

My heart sings when someone asks me if we have a bathroom.

Yeah, I think it's kind of a law.

I want to do somersaults when they ask me if I know where it is.

Three years working here and I'm still looking.

I love the stupid question. It makes my day when someone asks me if we have a menu.

No, the menu items are passed down by the village elders and recited verbally from generation to generation.

After I tell them we do, I especially like it when they ask me what's on it.

Should I recite it for you in its entirety?

How many wings come in a dozen?

46.

How do you cook your steaks, got a grill or something?

No, we use lasers.

Do you live here?

No, I commute from California.

Are you open?

No, the doors are open and we are all here in uniform because it's how we like to spend our days off.

I can't get enough of them. Keep them coming, people. It makes my night and fills my head with joyful bliss. Please come to my oceanfront bar and ask me what time the dolphins come swimming by.

Not sure. They didn't drop off their schedules this week.

It's one of my guilty pleasures. My only complaint is the stupid questions I get aren't imaginative enough. Yeah, "How big is your 9-ounce filet" is good, but how about, "How many chews in gum?" "How many cuts in a knife?" "Is a dog's mouth really cleaner than a human's?"

It's time to step up your game, people. Let's see what you've got for me.

The biggest problem with stupid questions is they usually rear their ugly heads at the worst possible time. It usually happens when we are at our busiest and it almost always puts us in the weeds.

By the way, "weeds" is an industry term. It pretty much means that you are running behind (usually because of some moron) and will spend the next however long trying to catch up.

If your server or bartender is sweating profusely or breathing heavily when he or she approaches your table, he is in the weeds. If, while she is speaking with you, she is constantly glancing over to her other tables, she in the weeds. If it's a busy night and you say something dumb that will keep him at your table for much longer than necessary, he is so far in the weeds it would take a machete to get him out.

At the Freedom Steakhouse and Brewery, we only served four

bottled beers. This was a never-ending source of trauma to the various dorks who wandered through our front door. Many of these people took it as a personal insult that we didn't carry Busch Light. The fact that we were a brewery never seemed to register with them.

When someone asked what we carried in bottles, I would rattle off the four beers we stocked.

"Budweiser, Mich Light, Mich Ultra, and Miller Lite."

Nine out of ten times, the next words out of their mouths would be, "Bud Light."

"Budweiser, Mich Light, Mich Ultra, and Miller Lite."

"Coors Light."

Here's another one. If the bar or restaurant you are in does not have, or is out of, the beer you prefer, do not pretend to have an invisible knife and pantomime stabbing yourself in the chest repeatedly. This only serves in convincing your server or bartender that you are the king of all nerds.

There is also no reason to cry, scream, or throw a hissy-fit in this scenario. If you are old enough to drink, you should be old enough to conduct yourself like an adult when receiving such bad news.

Trying to make your server or bartender feel guilty by telling them that you drove all the way from Kalamazoo, does no good, either. If we tell you we are out, we are really out. There are none hidden in the back and it is not part of any conspiracy designed to deny you what you want. No matter what you say, your server or bartender cannot make one magically appear.

This said, I think I should also point out that your server or bartender does not do the ordering for the bar or restaurant. When you decide to rip them a new one because they don't have Stroh's Extra Light, you are yelling at the wrong person. They have nothing to do with it. At least call over a manager to yell at. They probably didn't have anything to do with it either, but they don't have five other tables to get to and you won't put them in the weeds.

I had this lady ask me for lemonade once and I politely informed her that we didn't serve lemonade at the Freedom Steakhouse and Brewery.

She asked me if I was sure.

I assured her that I had worked there for quite some time, and if there was indeed any lemonade on the premises, I would probably know about it.

Next she asked me *why* we didn't serve lemonade, and she didn't ask in a pleasant tone.

Are there actually people out there who believe the servers and bartenders have anything to do with deciding what is served at the restaurants they work? Do they think the Pizza Hut people sat down with their servers and said, "What do you think? Should we go with the pizza thing or what?"

We just work there. We had nothing to do with the planning designing or execution of what the place is all about.

At the hotel bar, the restrooms are located outside our bar. You simply walk out, into the lobby, and down a short flight of stairs. It's probably a twenty-second walk.

You have no idea what an incredible source of aggravation this is to some of my customers. They will huff and puff, throwing down their napkins, and storming out the door like I just insulted their mothers.

Gee, I'm sorry. I don't know why I didn't think of your laziness when I was designing the hotel.

While I'm on the subject, we don't cook your food, either. When your steak comes out overdone or undercooked, or your fish is too dry, or your fries are too cold, it is not my fault. I will do whatever I can to remedy the situation, but yelling at me really doesn't do any good. Don't waste your breath. I'm probably not listening, anyway.

Believe it or not, no one in the entire restaurant wants to screw you over. We want you to go away happy so that there is a chance you'll come back. That's how we make our money. If all our customers walked out pissed off, we wouldn't be in business for very long.

If there is something wrong with your meal, simply explain the situation to your server. They will get the problem resolved and there is no reason for anyone to go ballistic. Life is too short to get into a screaming match over a piece of meat.

I wish I was making this up, but I've had people in my face, acting like they want to throw down, because the bacon on their burger wasn't crispy the way they like it.

Say it, don't spray it, big boy.

All that said, if there is a problem with your meal or something wasn't done the way you wanted, by all means, don't be afraid to speak up. I do not take it as a personal insult if your steak is not cooked enough. Again, I want you to have a pleasant experience at my place. If you're happy, there is a good chance I'm going to make better money. If I make better money, I'm happy, too.

My favorites are the passive aggressive bozos who try to make you feel bad. After complaining about their meal, they are beyond being consoled, and nothing you say or do will make them happy.

"I could have them do another one or I'd be happy to get you a menu so you could choose something else."

"No! I'm not hungry anymore," they say as they throw their napkin over their plate and motion for you to take it away.

Like I said before, I will do whatever I can to fix these situations … to a point. After that, I really don't give a rat's ass. Do they think I really care whether or not they eat?

You could go on a thirty-day hunger strike for all I care. I'm not losing any sleep over it. The truth is, I probably couldn't pick you out of a lineup ten minutes after you've left my place.

No wonder people in the restaurant business drink.

This is the part where I'm going to tell you about all those horror stories you've heard, the things waiters and cooks do to get revenge on people who treat them bad.

We've all heard the stories about servers spitting in people's pasta or adding other bodily fluids to a person's meal. Dropping their food on the floor and or doing other disgusting things to it before serving it up with a smile.

There was a particularly good one going around for years that if you added a few drops of Visine into someone's drink it would give them a severe case of diarrhea. I have even heard of bartenders keeping a bottle behind the bar for just this purpose.

In all my years in the business, I can honestly say I have never done anything like this to anyone. No matter how tempting it might be at times. In fact, I have never even witnessed it happen before. Not once.

All those horror stories are merely urban legend. I'm not saying it has *never* happened, but you can be reasonably confident that no one is screwing with your food before you eat it.

Of course, when I find myself as a customer in a restaurant I make sure not to give my server any reason to mess with my food, but that's just me.

If I'm making it seem like every person who walks through the door of a restaurant is a total dweeb and an unbearable ass, I apologize. The truth is most people are very polite and nice. They just aren't any fun to talk about.

You know what they say about the squeaky wheel getting the oil. That's just the way it works.

The bad apples always mess it up for the good eggs.

OverMore than two-thirds of the people I wait on are friendly and considerate and I have no problem dealing with them at all. Although, if one more of these friendly people tells me there is a hole in their glass (ha ha), my head might explode.

Over the years, many of these people have elevated themselves up and beyond the status of mere customers. There are those I consider friends. Some of them I even see socially outside of work, while others I only see across the bar, but they are all friends just the same. This is one of the best things about my job.

I could fill a book with the names of the friends I've made in this business over the years, it just wouldn't be as funny to write about.

These are the people who make what I do bearable. They are

the people who you can take off to the side and tell about the jerk you're waiting on at table 404. They're the ones who are always ready with a joke or a smile, and they are the ones (along with my coworkers) who make what I do enjoyable. They are much more than just customers. They are a part of our family.

I will leave you with one more story before moving on to the next chapter.

In front of the Freedom Steakhouse and Brewery, there was an outside area with tables covered by an awning. We called this area the beer garden and NO, it's not where they grow the beer.

So, I'm working out there and I have this guy in a suit sitting at my table and looking at a menu. He was kind of snotty and was basically treating me like I was the monkey boy at the carnival freak show.

"How big are your pizzas?" he asked me (again with the pizza).

"Ten inches," I told him.

"How big is that?"

I couldn't resist. I held up two fingers about an inch apart and said, "It's about ten of those."

CHAPTER THREE
MULLETS AND MOHAWKS

I was originally going to call this chapter, *Preconceived Notions for People on the Go.*

My idea was to list every stereotype I could think of, generalizing different groups of people into ridiculous categories, so people who are too busy to do it themselves might have some sort of reference guide.

Stereotyping is something we are all guilty of to some extent. As our society evolves and we become more tolerant of others, we have begun to look past the typical stereotypes that were embraced for generations, but they still raise their ugly heads from time to time. Again, it's one of those human nature things. Even I'm guilty of it.

This particular human behavioral pattern is alive and well at your local bar or restaurant. Your bartender or server has a preconceived notion of the kind of person you are as soon as you sit down. This preconceived notion has been derived after hundreds (maybe thousands) of hours dealing with all sorts of people in all kinds of situations. You are typecast into your category within seconds of sitting down.

Is this fair? Of course not.

Is it accurate? I would say it's a very precise science with a 90 percent chance of error. People do it just the same.

I'm sure it happens to me wherever I go. When I walk into a bar or restaurant, I know exactly what people are thinking.

"Oh, he's so good looking, he's got to be stuck up."

"That guy looks so intelligent, he is going to make me feel intellectually inferior."

"That guy is so cool-looking, I feel like such a nerd."

Just because people think things doesn't make them true. I, for example, am not stuck up.

We all do this to various degrees. The problem with doing it in my business is it can cost you money. In the restaurant industry, the way you treat people has a direct effect on the amount of money you take home. You would be surprised at how many servers or bartenders don't understand this simple premise.

One of the things I've learned along the way is if you consistently prejudge and expect the worst from people, they will rarely let you down. It is a self-fulfilling prophecy.

If you automatically assume someone is going to be a certain way, you have biased yourself toward him or her and, as such, you have dictated not only the way you perceive him or her, but the way you treat that person, as well. When you do this, you are also dictating the way this person will treat you in return. You have turned him or her into exactly what it was you decided you didn't like about him or her in the first place.

In this country, you have every right to like or dislike anything or anyone you want and for whatever reason you want. What you can't do is discriminate. In this business, it is not only illegal, but it's a certain path to poverty. If you plan to do it in this industry, you had better stock up on Ramen noodles, because it's all you're going to be able to afford.

A perfect example of this happened while I was still working at the Crustacean House.

It was late in the evening, and the restaurant was winding down. After working a double shift, a girl I worked with (we will call her Rhoda) was seated what would surely be her last table of the evening. It was a family of five and they were black. Rhoda went ballistic and complained to a manager. Not only was she upset because she was being sat again after her long shift, but she was angry because she was being seated a table of black people and she was positive they were not going to leave a decent tip for her efforts. I don't think she had even approached the table before coming to this conclusion, so this assumption was based purely on the color of their skin.

The Crustacean House manager asked Rhoda if she was refusing to wait on the table because of their skin color. Rhoda replied that she had no problem waiting on black people throughout her shift, but it was unfair to give her this table at the end of her double, as it was common knowledge black people were notoriously bad tippers.

The Crustacean House manager asked her again. "Are you saying you refuse to wait on the table because they're black?"

Rhoda said yes. She was fired on the spot.

I wasn't there when this happened. I was already off work and was sitting with another coworker named Suki. We were having a beer at the Freedom Steakhouse and Brewery, as it was one of our hangouts before I began working there.

Suki happened to be a good friend of Rhoda's.

Rhoda came storming into Freedom with tears running down her face, explaining how she had been wrongfully terminated. She told us the whole story, everything that was said between her and the manager, just as I've laid it out here.

Suki comes from a biracial family. Her mother is Korean and her father is black. She was one of those exotic beauties with a unique look, but there was no mistaking from which parent she inherited her pigmentation.

"Are you kidding me?" Suki finally said. "You are actually going to sit here and tell me this story like you didn't deserve to be fired?"

Rhoda was dumbfounded. "You know how black people tip."

"I'm black and you've been out with me. Do I tip poorly?"

"Of course not."

For the next twenty minutes, I sat there and watched in shock as the two went back and forth. Rhoda was arguing how she had been wronged, trying to justify herself, explaining how it didn't make her racist. Suki tried to explain how her actions were offensive, but Rhoda stood by her guns. Fed up, Suki finally got up and walked out.

I heard later the table in question turned out to be very pleasant and left a good tip.

See what I mean about prejudging?

This is one of the more blatant examples of what I'm talking about, but it happens all the time. Your bartender or server is like everybody else in the world. Many of them have become quite adept at coming to these preconceived notions, bringing their own prejudices and stereotypes from whatever walk of life they come from. If they are good at what they do, you will never be the wiser.

Let's go ahead and get this out of the way. Here's an easy-to-use reference guide for people who aren't very good at lumping large groups into convenient categories, pigeon-holing them for their own, narrow-minded bigotry. It's fun for the whole family.

Keep in mind, I'm not making this up. I have heard every one of these, over the years.

1. Black people. No need to cover this one. Rhoda already took care of that.

2. Anyone Jewish is ... well, that's just too easy.

3. If you have two or more women together with no men, you are guaranteed a bad tip. Women are, by nature, the cheapest skinflints on the planet. They make Jewish people look like extravagant spenders. This is a rule every person in the restaurant business knows to be true, even if it is completely false.

4. Anyone from a foreign country is a terrible tipper. It doesn't matter what country, as it's much easier to lump the entire rest of the world together as one. Anyone who speaks another language or speaks with a foreign accent can be placed in this category. If you don't hear a person speak, it is perfectly acceptable to place them in this category for merely looking foreign.

5. Anyone under the age of 22 will run you to death and

leave a bad tip. Young people just suck. They also play their music too loud.

6. Anyone over the age of 65 will run you to death and leave a bad tip. Experts believe this is partially because many people of age don't realize, while a shiny nickel was a pretty good tip in 1931, it is no longer the big deal it once was. They will also spend most of the evening complaining about anything and everything. Of course, your own grandparents are exempt from this rule.

7. Rednecks are the most demanding, cheapest people on the face of the earth and nothing you can do will ever make them happy. You have a better chance of discovering a new animal species at the mall than of getting a good tip from a redneck. For the benefit of anyone who does not live in the Redneck Riviera, like me, and does not have regular contact with rednecks, I have devised a quick checklist to use so you can recognize a redneck when you see one.

   A redneck would be anyone who:

   a. has a mullet.

   b. wears a NASCAR hat or T-shirt.

   c. wears overalls.

   d. drinks Natural Light in a can.

   e. orders a Dickel and Dew (George Dickel and Mountain Dew).

   f. does not fit the mold of what you think they should look like.

   *For the record, I grew up outside Baltimore City and I

would place the Rednecks of Glen Burnie, Maryland way above these South Carolina posers.

8. When waiting on other servers or bartenders, there is a 50 percent chance they will either be very easy and tip extremely well or they will be super demanding and horrible tippers. There is no in-between when it comes to this rule and it will always be one extreme or the other.

This, of course, was just a quick guide and a small sampling of the possibilities and, as I said earlier, there is a 90 percent chance of error with everything stated above, but that's kind of the point to the whole deal.

If you are a bartender or server, feel free to use my list to prejudge your potential customers as you see fit, just be prepared to go home broke.

The point is, if you want to be good at this, you have to treat everyone who sits at your bar or in your section in the same way. After they have proven they suck, you can hate them all you want, no matter who they are.

On a related side note involving rednecks, one of the girls I work with at the Big Digs told me a great one. She worked at a restaurant in the same complex as the Freedom Steakhouse and the Crustacean House. I have no connection to this restaurant at all, so who cares if I use the name? It's called Landry's. Sue away.

She told me she and her coworkers during the busy summer months had a game they liked to play called Redneck Bingo. Each server was given a card with five items on it. It was a bit like a scavenger hunt, but instead of going out and searching for an item, you had to wait for the item to come to one of the tables in your section. Each thing was assigned a letter. The first server to spell BINGO won.

Some of the items included were things like:

B- Anyone who asks for a Mr. Pibb

I- Any table with four Mountain Dews

N- Anyone wearing an Affliction or Tap Out T-shirt

G- Any table that gets five or more sides of ranch dressing

O- Anyone who asks for a Busch or Natural Light beer

Too funny.

Hey, I said you had to treat people fairly. I never said you couldn't have some fun at their expense.

I didn't intend this chapter to be what makes a good server, but it seems to be the direction we're heading, so let's run with it.

First things first. I should point out, like most people who work in this business, I am a magnet for bad service. I do not know why this is, but it is almost a given that whenever I go to a new restaurant or bar, I receive horrible service. Maybe it's why I tend to go back to the same places. It is also possible that my standards are a bit higher than others, as well.

One night, I took my kids to a popular pizza place in town. We ordered three of those small, one-person pizzas and an order of bread sticks. The kids got plain cheese pizzas and I got one of those meat lover deals. Our server disappeared for fifteen minutes, during which time we all needed refills on drinks. When she showed up, she dropped off the pizzas but no breadsticks and ran off before we could get more drinks.

My kids' pizzas were right on the money, but mine came out with green peppers and black olives. Not the meatiest of meats.

It took me forever to flag her down. When she finally came by, I explained how we needed drinks, never got our breadsticks and received the wrong pizza. I was calm and polite while explaining the situation.

The girl pulled out her pad and read over her notes. She then turned it toward me, so I could read it, and pointed out that she had no mention of breadsticks and that her pad *clearly* read vegetarian pizza.

You realize I'm not the one who wrote that, right?

I explained to her that I have never ordered anything vegetarian in my life and that I wasn't trying to be a problem, but I just wanted to get some breadsticks and a pizza with some animal flesh on it.

She eventually got it all fixed. I should also mention there were two other tables in the entire restaurant, so it wasn't like she was in the weeds or anything. I still left her a good tip, but I'm stupid that way.

That's a pretty good example of the service I tend to attract when I go out to eat. To be fair, when I go back to the places I frequent regularly, I generally get great service.

So, if you currently work in the restaurant industry or are considering entering the restaurant industry, here are some rules to follow if you don't want to suck at what you do.

1. As I've already stated, treat people fairly no matter what you might think of them when you first see them.

2. Look around you.

This might seem like such a simple thing, but I see it wherever

I go. The bartender will be leaning on the bar, talking to someone, or looking up at the TV, never glancing around to see if anyone needs anything. People could be dying of thirst or choking to death four stools down, and these people would remain oblivious. Their blinders are securely in place and they have no idea what's going on around them. I have been in bars where you need a flare gun to get a drink.

I'm fond of telling people I can share with the secret to being a great bartender. When they question me further, I like to demonstrate this top-secret skill, the one that separates the mediocre bartenders from the true professionals. To do this, I simply turn my head from one side to the other, looking around as I do.

It's as simple as that, and a large percentage of people who do what I do just don't get it.

I should also point out that while this behavior by your bartender or server is annoying, it does not give you the right to take drastic measures. Even in this scenario, if you bang your empty glass on the bar, you are scum.

3. Do not assume that just because I am sitting at your bar or in your section I want to be your best friend. There are things I don't need to know about you. Not everyone who comes to your place is lonely and looking for companionship. Some of us just want to get a beer and watch the game.

If I am looking for someone to talk to, I will most likely send out some sort of signal. A good bartender is receptive without being overbearing. This has a lot to do with your ability to read people and this is probably something that no one can teach you. If it's a skill you don't have, you may be able to acquire it over time if you sit back and observe instead of talking constantly. In most cases, being friendly and making yourself available will be more than sufficient. If we strike up a friendship, that is great too, but make sure I'm looking for a friend. When you force yourself on me, it just annoys me.

4. This one is probably pretty close to rule number three, but it is entirely possible that you are not as funny or charming as you and your friends think you are. Please do not go out of your way to entertain me, unless I am giving you a vibe that says otherwise.

I am probably not there for a comedy routine unless, of course, you work at a comedy club and, in this case, I will wait for the show to begin. There is nothing worse than having to pretend to be amused out of politeness while secretly just wanting your bartender or server to leave you alone and go get you a drink.

I realize there are people out there who are very funny and whom I would probably love to listen to while they were waiting on me. If you are a one of these people, feel free to feel me out and take it from there. Just make sure you get my drink first.

It's all about reading people.

I always seem to end up with the older server sitting down at my table doing Henny Youngmen jokes for twenty minutes while I dream of a cold beverage.

Again, this isn't to say that you can't be friendly or even make a few wisecracks here and there. By all means, make me smile if you can. There's nothing like a few good zingers to get things rolling. Just don't monopolize my time and make me sit through a half-hour monologue on how bad your day was. I am getting older by the minute and I don't know how many good years I have left.

I was once in a bar with two friends, both women. I had some exciting news to tell them and I was in the midst of relaying my information in the form of a story, telling them how it all came about.

Three times while I was trying to tell my story, the bartender interrupted me to show us some various bar tricks he was quite proud of. These tricks involved him tossing around bar tins and bottles, flipping them in the air and catching them behind his back. By the third time, I was fuming. I remember one of my friends patting my leg, giving me a look that said, "Just relax. The dork will be finished with his stupid bar trick in a second."

While this guy was quite good when it came to the flair end of the bartending game, he was oblivious to the subtle skills of the trade, the ones that actually help you to make money.

5. One of the skills you will need to acquire if you plan on being successful in this business is the ability to fake sincerity. I can't emphasize enough how important this one is.

When I come to you and point out there's a chip in my glass, it is imperative you act like you give a good shit. If I am crying and whining because the extra butter I ordered with my baked potato did not come out with my meal, it is crucial that you pretend this is a life or death issue for you as well.

Of course, none of us really care beyond how it might affect our tip, but put on a good show. Let me see the concern on your face. Let me hear it in your voice.

Many people believe the acronym T.I.P.S. stands for *To* Insure *Proper Service,* but I believe it actually stands for *To* Insure *Phake Sincerity.*

Everyone on earth wants to know you feel their pain and empathize with their plight, no matter how stupid or unimportant their pain or plight might be. It is the bond that holds us together as a race.

6. If you wish to be successful in this field, it is also important that you *never* have a bad day. This means you can never be sad, depressed, or in a bad mood. You must always be happy, upbeat, and friendly, no matter what is going on in your life.

I realize this sounds like an impossible goal to achieve, but you would be surprised. It's not as hard as you think. It's kind of like that faking sincerity thing. A little practice and you will be fine. If you practice long enough, you will be one of the mindless zombie drones in no time, just like the rest of us.

Try it out on your significant other. Act like you're truly interested when your wife or girlfriend tells you about that thing that one girl said to her at work today, the one that got her so upset. Pretend you're genuinely thrilled when your boyfriend is talking about the four-game winning streak his favorite football team is on. These are probably things that you are already doing.

Along with this, you will need to develop the ability to appear to be listening to someone when they talk, even though you are actually making a grocery list in your head.

7. This one is a deal-breaker, so pay close attention. You will need to learn how to put up with people being rude and nasty without turning around and bitch-slapping them. Almost every restaurant in America frowns upon physical violence toward their guests, with the possible exception of a few biker bars I know.

It sounds obvious, but it is not always so easy.

In pretty much any situation, your management team will side with the customer in these scenarios, so pick your battles carefully. The one possible exception is if your customer gets violent with you first and then there is still no guarantee the restaurant will side with you. Usually the best way to handle these situations is to avoid violence at all costs.

In fact, it's pretty much a good idea to refrain from losing your temper all together. This can be extremely difficult at times, as people can be major assholes. They will go out of their way to push you to the limit. Basically, they do this because they are spineless dweebs who know you are powerless to do anything without the risk of losing your job.

By the way, if you are one of those spineless dweebs who enjoys berating your server because your garlic mashed potatoes aren't garlic-y enough, I should warn you, there are quite a few people in this business who don't value their jobs all that much. One day you will mess with the wrong person and go home with a black eye or worse.

A good rule of thumb is to never raise a hand against or touch a customer. You should also refrain from kicking, throwing things at, or putting a sleeper hold on anyone you are waiting on. Shouting at, cussing out, giving the finger, mooning, or sticking your tongue out at your customers are usually not the way to go, either.

If you are still confused, go back and see rules 5 and 6.

At this point, I need to go into another area that needs discussing. The kind of bar you work at can dictate how much of this list you will need to adhere to.

If you work at a large corporate chain or high-profile bar, you need to follow this list to the letter.

If you work in a neighborhood bar where you pretty much know everyone and are good friends with the owner, you can probably bend these rules as you need to.

If you are a really hot girl who tends bar at a strip club, you can pretty much throw all of these rules out the window and do whatever you want.

If you are a really hot girl who tends bar at a night club, you can pretty much throw all of these rules out the window and do whatever you want.

Okay, now that's out of the way, let's look at your server or bartender from the customer's side. These are things you should know about your servers or bartenders to help understand them and dictate how you should interact with them.

I should preface this by saying, like most of this book, these rules do not apply to everyone in this business and in many ways are a lot like the generalizations and preconceived notions we talked about earlier. So, with that in mind, here we go.

There is a very good chance that your server or bartender:

- is VERY hung over and was up quite late the night before. Whatever you do, don't speak too loudly. Your voice probably already sounds like you are speaking through a megaphone. Also, don't bring up anything that might remind your bartender or server of how sick and queasy they actually feel. Some topics to avoid are raw animal guts, old seafood, and that clump of spices you sometimes find at the bottom of the Doritos bag.

- is stoned out of his or her mind. This is certainly not the rule of thumb, but depending on the bar or restaurant you find yourself in, this could very well be the case. Am I saying that all bartenders and servers are potheads? Of course not. In fact, the ratio of dope smokers in the restaurant business is probably not much greater than that of any other American industry. In every restaurant there is always that one guy (or girl) who goes off to the bathroom or out back by the dumpster and comes back mellower and in a really good mood. This does not necessarily mean they are off getting high. There is a very good chance they just went off to do some inspirational reading and have come back renewed and revitalized and with some really red and glassy eyes.

- does not remember where they left their car last night. After work they probably *went to some bar where they heard about this really cool party and they got a ride with some girl they just met and afterwards they ended up back at her apartment and … okay, you get the idea.

- is in the middle of some very heavy drama involving his or her girlfriend or boyfriend and the fact that you want extra sour cream on your baked potato does not interest him or her all that much.

- is trying to figure out how they spent 94 dollars the night before.

- does not understand why they are constantly getting screwed on their schedule when it is so obvious that they are the hardest worker and best employee in the restaurant.   *is totally checking out your date's cleavage (this one mostly applies to male servers and bartenders).

- is totally checking out your date's ass when she gets up to use the ladies' room (again this mostly applies to the males).

This would be a good time to point out if you are a hot woman and you are in a bar or restaurant, you are pretty much the main topic of discussion of all the men who work there. I know this may seem a bit sexist and uncouth, but that is only because it is. If you happen to be wearing something low cut or an extremely short skirt, you are the *only* topic of conversation. What can I say? We are guys. I don't know if this is true for women, as I have never been one, but I suspect it might also be true. I know I have caught many of the girls I've worked with undressing me with their eyes over the years.

- would rather be somewhere else.

While I was working on the latest list, I thought of another story. It happened while I was working at O'Brady's and it involves rule number 2.

I should begin by saying that I've never been much of a weed smoker. Over the years, I have messed with it from time to time, but it's never really been my thing. For one, I can't do it in public because it makes me way too stupid.

So, I'm working at O'Brady's and it's like 10:30 on a Sunday night and the place is dead. I have one customer named Eddie, who is a friend of mine, and he's drinking a screwdriver (vodka and orange juice).

Eddie has been my sole customer for the past two hours and we've been sitting around watching TV and shooting the breeze. Eddie asks me if I want to get stoned.

"No, I can't do that. I'm working," I say.

Eddie looks around the empty room. "Who's going to know?"

"You know what? What the hell!"

So we go down to the back dining room where those infamous

picnic tables were (I got a lot of use out of those tables) and we smoke some marijuana. I think I might have taken two or three hits.

We go back up to the bar and I am shit-faced. I mean stoned beyond belief. I can barely function.

At 11 o'clock, the Southern District Police station in Baltimore City has its shift change and they all decide to stop in to O'Brady's for a beer. So, I've got like twelve cops sitting at my bar and my buddy and I are completely wiped out.

Eddie, of course, thinks this is hilarious and he's sitting at the bar, giggling like a schoolgirl. I, on the other hand, am paranoid beyond words and am totally convinced that every cop there knows exactly what I've been doing. I keep going down to Eddie and saying things like, "Be cool," or "Keep it together." Eddie just laughs.

Eventually Eddie finishes his drink and orders another. I am totally freaked out that my friend would have the nerve to do something as crazy as order another drink while I'm in the midst of a meltdown and positive I will end up in jail before the night is over.

I take his glass, turn around and make his drink, setting it back down in front of him.

"What's this?" he asks.

I look down at his glass, realizing I have merely poured a shot of vodka into it. Then, I look up at Eddie in horror. "Are you *trying* to get me arrested?"

"Can I get some orange juice?"

Reluctantly, I take his glass and add OJ to it, slamming it down in front of him.

"How about some ice?" Eddie asks, barely controlling the laughter fit that has overcome him.

"You're killing me," I tell him as I take his glass and add ice.

I didn't go to jail that night and, as far as I know, none of the police officers at the bar even suspected I was high as a kite. Maybe they just didn't care, one way or the other. Either way, it was the last time I ever got stoned at work.

Drinking behind the bar is another story. To be honest, I don't drink at work anymore. This is mainly because I think being drunk at work is a miserable feeling. Besides making me tired and lazy, and the night drags on forever, it's never a good idea to be drunk while dealing with people and money.

After I left O'Brady's, I got a job at another bar called the Hull Street Blues Café. That is the real name of the bar and I see no reason to make up a fake one. The owner, is a good guy and I don't think he'll sue me.

I worked there for quite a while, and it was one of my most favorite jobs ever. The owner, Danny, was a good guy to work for, most of the time, and it was a fun working environment. It had a great atmosphere, a terrific clientele, and the staff was like family. We were always doing things together and most of us hung out there on our days off, coworkers and customers alike.

We had live music three nights a week, and many of the people who frequented Hull Street were servers and bartenders from other bars and restaurants around Baltimore. Danny had no problem with us drinking behind the bar. In fact, we were encouraged to let customers buy us drinks. I think we were supposed to wait until after nine or ten to begin drinking, and we were expected to never get wasted. Often times, Danny would be right there with us while we were having beers. It was like a non-stop party you got paid to attend.

Some of the fondest work memories I have are from the years I worked at Hull Street and, ironically, I can't think of a single story I could fit into this book. Most of the things that come to mind involve drunken debauchery and late-night parties with coworkers. Maybe this is another argument against drinking at work.

However you look at it, drinking behind the bar happens everywhere and there is a very good chance you have been served by someone who didn't remember serving you an hour later. That's just the way it is.

I have been in bars where the bartender has been falling down drunk and, to be honest, it's usually not much fun to witness. It usually doesn't do much in way of boosting the level of service, either.

I was in a bar once where they had a male and female bartender working together. The male may have been the owner or manager (I'm not sure). Apparently, the guy had been feeding shots and drinks to the girl for the entire night, as she could barely stand by the time my friend and I got there. The guy was leaning on the bar and taking our drink order when he asked us if we wanted to see something.

"Sure."

"Hey, Mary, show these guys."

At that, the very attractive drunk girl lifted her shirt and showed us her very large breasts. Classy, huh?

I don't actually remember if her name was Mary or not. I'm guessing it probably wasn't.

Anyway, I think this story represents the very best and worst of what I'm talking about. On one hand, I am a red-blooded American man who enjoys seeing a nice pair of cans as much as the next guy. On the other hand, there is something kind of wrong about taking advantage of a poor young drunk girl who obviously has self-esteem issues.

I don't think I ever got *that* drunk while I was at Hull Street, but maybe I just don't remember. Mary probably doesn't remember showing me her breasts, either.

It seems to me that I was always under control at work, but that's kind of how alcohol works, isn't it? Maybe it's why I can't think of any good Hull Street stories to include here.

Now that I think about it, I do remember sitting at the bar during my shift while my little sister and her friend waited on customers and washed glasses. Neither my sister, nor her friend, were ever employed at Hull Street Blues. I guess that wasn't such a good idea. Sorry, Danny.

Danny liked to sit around and talk about bars. He would sometimes talk about the restrictions and regulations the government was placing on bars and how it was making it difficult for many of them to keep their doors open. As part of his argument, he always said the American Revolution was born in a bar. I mention this because, years later, I happened to be reading a book by Wayne Curtis called *And a Bottle of Rum: The History of the New World in Ten Cocktails.* It's a wonderful book and I highly recommend it. He writes of the revolutionary times when taverns had become "de facto community centers, virtual Petri dishes for the breeding of a discontent that taverners learned to channel."

There you go. I always knew he was right, but when I read it, it made me think of Danny and of Hull Street.

Have you ever watched the show "Cheers"? I can tell you working in a bar is exactly like that. It is also nothing like that. I guess it makes as much sense as the generalizations and rules I gave you earlier. Maybe the number one rule would have to be that there are no rules and if there were, they would all be made to be broken at any given time.

My favorite episode of "Cheers" was when Woody was in the bartending contest and had to make all the crazy drinks. It's been forever since I've seen it and I may be recalling it completely incorrectly.

He is told to make a Screaming Viking.

"Would you like the cucumber bruised or not bruised?" he replies.

That pretty much sums up everything you need to know about bartenders, or maybe it's just a funny line from an old TV show.

The main thing you need to know is everyone is different, even if you lump them all in the same group, and that's why you have to treat them all exactly the same. This is true for customers as well as servers and bartenders.

Take notice the next time you go out to eat and I think you will see that I'm 100 percent correct. Either that, or you will find I am completely wrong. The important thing is to have fun with it and enjoy the ride.

I realize that I've called this chapter *Mullets and Mohawks,* but I have barely mentioned mullets and I haven't talked about mohawks at all. The truth is, I just liked the way it sounded and I thought it kind of spoke of the way we perceive the differences in people. Let's take a second to talk about mohawks.

When did the mohawk become the hairstyle of choice with boys under the age of seven? And where did this faux-hawk thing come from?

The mohawk was once the proud insignia of misfits, non-conformists, and rebels from the punk generation. They were worn with pride by some of the greatest punk rockers in history. Now, its bastard child is sported by Cub Scouts and stockbrokers, and it is the hairstyle of preference by people from middle America to the jet set scene. It just seems wrong, somehow. I guess I'm just a mohawk purist.

So, that said, just say no to drugs, especially if you have a bar full of cops, and keep the drinking at work to a minimum if you want to be able to recall the Hull Street years and not get attacked by sharks. Be kind to your bartender, because he is probably hung over as hell and fighting with his girlfriend. Watch out for the rednecks and foreigners, and if you find yourself in a bar and a guy leans over and asks you if you want to see something, tell Mary I said hi.

I will end this chapter with this. One day I was working at the Freedom Steakhouse and Brewery and I approached the table of a young couple. They were attractive and well-dressed and seemed to be in a deep conversation.

As I got there I heard the guy say, "You and him's relations, ain't ya?"

"Yeah, we's kin," she answered.

You just never know.

CHAPTER FOUR

MY BOTTOMLESS CUP RUNNETH OVER

How many loaves of bread do you need?

The Freedom Steakhouse and Brewery gives guests a free loaf of bread with dinner. In fact, I would pretty much give a loaf to anyone who asked.

You would not believe how many loaves of free bread some people can eat. I understand it's free, but give me a break. Just because you're not paying for it doesn't mean you need to go for the record. I would have loved to go home and have dinner with some of those people just to see how many loaves of Wonder Bread they went through with each meal. I'm guessing not a lot. They have to pay for Wonder Bread.

And ranch dressing. Whoever invented ranch dressing, I hate their guts. Don't get me wrong, I like the taste of it. Who doesn't? But if you need to douse everything you eat in ranch dressing, you have a serious problem. I'm guessing you have food issues that stem back to childhood. Maybe you just hate the taste of all foods and you need to hide it under the ranch.

It could be the Hidden Valley people have been secretly putting some sort of highly addictive chemical in the formula for all these years, creating a race of ranch-craving crackheads who will stop at nothing to get their product. In the not-so-distant future, we will all be wandering the streets and begging for change to support our ranch habits. Ranch-related crime sprees will be on the rise. Black market ranch dealers will be selling their product in back alleys and schoolyards.

Or maybe it isn't ranch dressing that you love so much, at all. Maybe it's FREE ranch dressing that makes your heart go pitter-pat.

The actual reason isn't nearly as fun and I am fairly certain that these people are not going through three loaves of bread and four bottles of Hidden Valley with every meal.

And guys, if you are on a date and she gets three sides of ranch dressing with her chicken fingers, she is sending you a clear message. The message is: *As soon as I'm married, I'm putting on ninety pounds.*

I'm not trying to be mean, but if your date can chug a bottle of ranch dressing, there might be some Weight Watchers in her future. Not that there is anything wrong with a bigger girl. I've always thought there is nothing sexier than a big girl who smells like cheese fries, but that's just me.

My point is, people love free stuff. I truly believe you could put a sign on the front of any restaurant advertising *Free Rocks*, and people would be lined up around the block. People are knuckleheads when it comes to free stuff. When you put four or more people together, their collective I.Q. drops 35 points. This is a proven fact. (I might be making that up, but it sure seems like it).

People lose their minds when it comes to free stuff. They don't know how to act. They lose all self-control and turn into raving maniacs. Take your refills on sodas and iced teas. I swear someone is going to explode at my work someday. They will just drink one too many free refills and there will be bits and pieces of cheapskate all over the restaurant. People will be washing particles of penny-pincher out of their hair for weeks.

Okay, it's free. We get it. That doesn't mean you have to make yourself sick on it.

It's like they're camels and they're storing liquids for a trek across the desert.

And how about these people who let their kids drink thirteen sodas with their meal? What are they thinking?

"Don't worry about Junior, Martha. It's free."

Yeah, it's free all right. It's also the same stuff people use to clean car batteries and your kid is working on his fourteenth. But he'll be fine.

Not to mention the nine-hour sugar/caffeine high the kid's going to be on.

Talk about your good parenting.

I don't get it much at the hotel bar, but I used to love it when people asked me if our cups had bottoms. What kind of question is that?

Of course they have bottoms. How else would they be able to hold liquids?

Now I understand what they were actually asking is if they had to pay for the 23 refills they intended to get, but what a stupid way to ask. Just once I would have liked to tell them we tried the cups without bottoms, but they made a terrible mess so we went back to the more conventional method of serving drinks.

My plan was to stop calling them refills and start calling them free-fills. I took my idea to my general manager and explained to him how this would increase the amount of sodas we moved on a regular basis.

He wasn't crazy about the idea. I think it had something to do with the fact that it would increase operating expenses without increasing profits in any way. Some people just don't see the big picture like I do.

No one is saying that asking for a refill of your drink makes you a bad person. We all get thirsty and it's certainly nice to have a cold drink to wash down your meal, but this doesn't mean it's okay to guzzle your Mountain Dew down as soon as your server sets it in front of you and then ask for another. Again, this goes back to me not having time to fetch stuff for my other tables if I have to keep fetching stuff for you every eight seconds.

I truly believe that some people just love to make other people do stuff for them. Some of them ask for stuff (especially free stuff) because they crave the satisfaction they get by making someone else do their bidding. Half of the time they don't even use it.

One day at Freedom, I went up to a table that sits by the side door and it was cracked open slightly. The girl next to the door said, "Shut that door, will ya?" She certainly could have shut it herself. It wasn't even a particularly complicated door. It would have merely required her to pull it shut. I'm not even sure she would have had to get out of her seat in order to reach it.

Are your hands painted on? You're closer to the door than I am. Get off your lazy ass and shut it your own damned self!

As you have probably figured out by now, the Freedom Steakhouse and Brewery wasn't exactly a fine dining establishment. Not that I'm knocking it. It was a cozy and friendly place with a comfortable atmosphere and good food. It was the kind of place where you can get up and shut the door and nobody is going to care, one way or the other.

If you are wondering how I handled the situation, I handled it the way any good server would. I shut the door.

People just like to be demanding. I was working a busy happy hour one day and the place was packed. This sweet, elderly couple came up and asked if I wouldn't mind making someone leave so they could have a place to sit.

Sure. Why not? How about if I snag their credit card so you don't have to worry about paying while I'm at it?

Slightly off the subject, I have to tell you this one. The same day as the door incident happened, a couple from out of town came in and another friend of mine was waiting on them. Like I said, it was a microbrewery and there were dozens of different beers we offered through out the year, many of them coming and going all the time. This couple had been in our place the year before and they were trying to remember which beer they had tried during their last visit. The guy actually said, "I can't remember what it was called, but I remember that it was kind of yellow."

Yellow? Beer? That's odd. Was it kind of wet and did it have white foamy bubbles floating on top?

The only stupid question is the unasked question? I don't think so.

Now, in their defense I will say that we did quite a few darker porters, stouts, browns, and reds. The blackberry wheat was actually sort of pink so the yellow description did eliminate a slew of possibilities. But, since most of the beers we made could be described as "yellow," it was pretty much impossible for my friend to figure out which beer they had sampled the year before. You have got to love dealing with the public.

I also really used to love the people who came into the bar 45 minutes before happy hour began.

"Can I get you something to drink?"

"What time does happy hour start?"

"Four o'clock."

Just like everywhere else in America.

"I'll wait."

I don't know about you, but I'm not sitting in a bar at an empty table for 45 minutes. How much of a loser do you have to be to do that in order to save a buck and a half?

My favorites were the ones who sat there empty-handed for three quarters of an hour, and then ordered a Diet Coke. Diet Coke is not on happy hour special and it costs the same all the time. What is going on in these people's minds?

Let's get back to free stuff.

Myrtle Beach, as I've told you, is a tourist town. Some people like to call it the Redneck Riviera.

The height of our off-season hits in January. It is (by far) the slowest time of the year. The time right after Christmas is pretty much the slowest for everyone in the restaurant business, but in a beach town it is magnified considerably.

To battle this, the Freedom Steakhouse and Brewery ran a promotion every January. Twice a week, throughout the entire month, they offered two-for-one dinners, buy one and get one of equal or lesser value for free.

Before I go any further, I should point out that the restaurant made very little money off this promo and, while it was very good advertising, they did it mostly to benefit the people who worked there, helping them get through the long winter. It was actually a very cool thing. Everyone in the restaurant business knows the one surefire way to fill your place is to give something away. It's just that there is very little profit in free stuff.

That said, let's talk about twofers.

You have never witnessed anything like it. Nothing short of surviving an actual battle could prepare a person for the carnage and violence that overtakes the restaurant during twofers. It is, simply put, the invasion of the blue hairs and it is a scary thing to live through.

Now, I want to go on the record as saying that I have nothing against senior citizens. I have known many wonderful elderly Americans throughout my life and I hope to one day join their ranks (God permitting).

I also fully understand that many retired people are living on fixed incomes and saving a large amount of money on a nice dinner is a big deal. There is nothing wrong with saving money. I'm all for it. Just keep things in perspective. It's a meal, not a winning Lotto ticket.

Maybe the best way to tell you about it is to describe a typical two-for-one night.

First off, the special started at 6 p.m., so the entire staff was in place by 4 p.m.

The first thing you notice is the total lack of wildlife of any kind. Flocks of birds scatter from trees and head as far away as they can get. Cats, dogs, and squirrels can be seen fleeing the area hours before it begins. Animals have a sixth sense when it comes to these things. It's another survival mechanism Mother Nature provides.

By 4:15, you begin getting that sickly feeling in the pit of your stomach, and you notice how quiet everything is. Too quiet. The world seems sedate and surreal.

This is when the theme from "Jaws" starts playing in the background.

At 4:29, the first group is spotted crossing the parking lot. They usually travel in even number groups. Two…four…six. They hunt better in even numbers.

"Battle stations! Everyone in place! We have Q-Tips approaching at twelve o'clock!"

There is a helpless sensation that comes over you as you watch them make their way toward you. Hobbling across the asphalt with their walkers and canes, you can already see that look in their eyes, and it sends a chill down your spine. It's a ruthless determination. The vicious and brutal look of a wild animal about to feed.

A numbness overtakes your body and you give in to the idea that your destiny is no longer in your own hands. Your fate, at this point, is in the hands of a higher being and, from here on out, you're just along for the ride. These people are going to eat cheap and there is no force on earth that can stop them.

By 4:30, they're everywhere. The line extends three blocks.

There are still ninety minutes before the twofers actually begin, but that doesn't phase the bargain hunters. They're ready to eat now and they consider you the one thing standing between them and their free meal. The low murmur and grumbling is getting louder.

The trick here is to never look them in the eye. This is when they're the most dangerous. One wrong move could be the difference between life and death. If you were to get too close, chances are, you'd find yourself on the business end of one of those walking sticks.

At least you're not working the hostess stand. That's where the real danger lies. If one of those girls were to turn her back on this angry mob, it would be over in seconds. Once they broke through the perimeter they would overtake us. The staff would be huddled together, in the back of the restaurant, fighting off the swarm of geriatric maniacs with knives and forks.

They look old, but they're quick and feisty when they're ready to feed. Before you could say "Geritol," the whole place would be a frenzied, bloody battle of survival.

The closer it gets to six o'clock, the meaner they get. Little old ladies are using language that not only makes you blush, but sends a cold chill down your spine. They're looking at you like you're on the menu.

By six, they have been waiting in line for an hour and a half. They're cold, tired, and hungry. Managers and hostesses are being knocked aside as they try to seat people at tables. It's hard to believe these are the same people who put $5 in their grandkids' birthday cards.

Four hundred and fifty people fill the main dining room, as well as the bar. Pandemonium isn't strong enough a word. Servers are running around like chickens with their heads cut off. The restaurant is crazier than an Attica prison riot.

You don't even want to go back in the kitchen. Food tickets are streaming out of the printer nonstop, and cooks are slapping slabs of meat onto the grill as fast as their arms allow. People are pouring frozen french fries straight out of the bag into the hot grease. Some of the kitchen staff will sweat off five pounds before it's over.

Back in the restaurant, all 450 of them are complaining.

"What's taking our food so long?"

Gee, I don't know. Maybe it's that 450 of you ordered at the same time?

Okay, I might be exaggerating slightly, but you'd probably be shocked by how close I actually came to how the twofers could be.

The lines sometimes extended out across the walkway, through the complex, and out into the parking lot, and our parking lot wasn't very close to the building. The line was ridiculous. I wouldn't wait in that line for a lap dance from Scarlett Johansen. Well, maybe for that I would, but not much else.

By the time they sit down to eat, they're pissed. Let me say that again. By the time they sit down to eat their FREE meal, they're pissed. They're pissed at me and they're pissed at the restaurant and they're pissed at the world.

This is what I used to love.

You are getting a free meal! What have you got to be pissed about?

Someone should do a study on what makes grumpy old men and women so grumpy. Certainly, once you have lived to be a certain age, you have earned the right to act anyway you bloody damn want. I just don't know why you would want to be a miserable jackass. If I make it that far, you won't be able to wipe the smile off my face.

Why they even bother to leave their houses, I have no clue.

Okay, I realize you're upset because iced tea costs $1.95, but you are getting a $25 steak for free. Do you think you could stop bitching at me?

Once again, I feel like I need to say that not everyone is like this. The truth is, most of the people are polite, courteous and grateful to be saving a few bucks. It's that whole bad apple thing again. It's the swarm of bad that overshadows the good and skews the way we see things.

Also, if I wrote about all of the nice things people do and say during a shift, this would be no fun to read.

We had many retired persons who frequented our restaurant regularly and most of them were wonderful, sweet people who I looked forward to seeing and talking with. They're just kind of boring to write about.

The other crazy thing about the two for ones was, by 8 p.m., it was over. At 8:05 you could come in and get a table with no wait and not have to deal with the lines or the crowd.

My theory was they needed to be home because "Matlock" began at 8 p.m., but I could be wrong. Maybe it was actually "Murder She Wrote."

I also used to love those people who had to tell me how much they loved our restaurant. "We come here every year," they'd tell me.

You know, we are open all year round. You don't have to wait for two-for-ones to come see us.

So, eight times a year we had to battle back the ungrateful and thrifty hordes in order to deliver them their-half priced meals. It was a pain in the ass and the tips you made during twofers were nowhere near what they should have been, but I don't necessarily blame the people for that. Most didn't know any better.

If you're getting anything for free, you should be tipping on what the bill *would* have been. After all, your bartender or server still does the same amount of work whether that second meal is paid for or not.

People just don't think about that, and why should they? As long as they're saving money, what do they care?

For us, it was January. It was better than nothing at all.

I will admit, I used to get a kick out of it when people would go to pay their check with a hundred dollar bill.

"I'm sorry, this is the smallest I have. Can you break this?"

Yes sir, this is a $5 million-a-year restaurant. I think we can make change for a hundred.

They would act like they were handing me a $10,000 bill. I realize that, back in the day, a saw note was a big deal, but things have changed a little since then. I can't help it, it always made me smile. People are funny.

While we're talking about our elderly patrons, there's another thing I'd like to bring up. For awhile, Life Behind Bars was a weekly column I did for a local restaurant website. I wrote it for about a year and I had a lot of fun with it.

I don't think the woman who ran the website ever really got my sense of humor. She was very nice about it, but she thought I crossed a lot of lines. Can you imagine?

Eventually, we agreed I wasn't a good fit for what she was trying to do and we parted ways.

During my run there, I received a lot of emails from readers. One day I got a letter from a local couple who ate out regularly and consistantly left a 20 percent gratuity.

They said they noticed, every so often, inconsistencies in their bills, being overcharged for items they didn't order or receive. They wondered if it might happen because they were senior citizens and their servers thought they wouldn't notice the discrepancies.

It's sad to think this practice goes on in any industry. At the very least it is gross negligence and at it's worst it is criminal fraud and a violation of a person's civil liberties. Not to mention, it's just plain wrong.

I will let you in on another one of those little secrets I like to spill. If you are a server or bartender who discriminates and or conspires to rob the people who pay your bills with their patronage you are beyond any kind of measurable stupid. Not only is there a special place reserved in hell for you, but you might as well cut the pockets out of your pants and let your money fall to the ground.

Like I said earlier, if you think you can look at a person and tell what they are likely to tip, you are, not only delusional, but the kind of dumb that dumb people make fun of. If you even consider taking advantage of someone due to their age or of anything else you perceive as weakness, you are the kind of dirty that makes pond scum look clean.

What kind of person would do such a thing? Don't you have parents or grandparents? Don't you hope to one day join the ranks of elderly Americans? I can only guess Karma is licking her lips, biding her time with baited breath, waiting for the day you become AARP eligible.

Let's talk about more weird people.

You have to love pointers. These are people who are somehow afraid to speak the menu items out loud and simply point to whatever it is they want.

This is a pain in the ass as, chances are, I can't actually read what you're pointing at from where I'm standing. I am forced to lean over your shoulder and strain to read the small print under your fat finger. It would be so much quicker and easier if you could just tell me what you want.

I guess I'm taking it for granted that they can actually read. Maybe they're just pointing at random menu items, hoping they get something good.

Same-siders are weird, too. These are the people who don't

want to sit across from each other in the traditional dining method and opt to both sit on the same side of the table. This freaks me out. I don't get this at all. The entire balance of the table has been compromised and utter and total chaos and anarchy are sure to follow. I can only guess that these people cannot stand the thought of looking at each other while they eat.

But, it does remind me of a joke.

Jesus walks into a restaurant and goes up to the maitre d'. He says, "I need a table for 26."

The maitre d' looks back and says, "But I only count thirteen of you."

"Yeah," Jesus responds. "But we're all planning on sitting on the same side of the table."

You've got to love a joke that combines religion and restaurants.

And how about table hoppers...

This isn't Duck, Duck, Goose. Do you really need to try out every table in the restaurant? Trust me, I speak from experience when I say that all of them are pretty much the same.

It's like Goldie Locks and the Three Bears. *This table is too hard and this table is too soft, but this table is just right.*

It's a table!

Speaking of tables, if you walk into a restaurant and there are five empty tables and one of them is dirty, why would you sit down at the dirty table? This happens all the time and it drives me crazy.

Oh yeah, and I *really* love the people who want to go through everything you carry, asking the price of everything.

"How much for an order of french fries?"

"Three dollars."

"Mashed potatoes?"

"Three dollars."

"Kettle chips with sea salt?"

"Three dollars."

It gets old after a half an hour or so, especially with all my other tables staring me down, waiting to ask how much fries cost.

And I love the people who get angry with me because they think the prices are too high.

"Three dollars for french fries? That's insane! It's highway robbery!"

Once again, I don't set the prices.

While I have your attention, let me mention another thing that makes me absolutely crazy. After I take your credit card and run it, I will bring back the receipt for you to sign and I will drop it off with a pen. Please do not be that dip-shit who steals my pen. I need that pen to take dinner orders and to give it to other customers so they can sign their credit card receipts. If you need a pen that bad, go buy your own or go steal one from the bank like normal Americans. The thing is, I can't go to the store and buy another pen because I'm stuck at work. If everyone comes in and steals my pens I am screwed for the night.

Here's one: If you want a glass of water, by all means ask for it, but don't be the jackass who orders a round of waters for everyone. There is nothing worse than finishing up a drink order and the last guy says, "And give us all a glass of water."

Way to go, Mr. Big Spender.

I understand that in many restaurants you will automatically receive a glass of water with your meal. Usually in these restaurants there will already be a water glass out as part of the table setting. I worked in a brewery. When you asked me for a glass of water, I used to put it in a pint glass.

If your friends want a glass of water, they can ask for it themselves and I will be happy to get one for them, but I guarantee I will be throwing out 90 percent of those waters you ordered after you leave. You are simply wasting my time and energy and no one is impressed. If you want to impress somebody, order a round of shots.

Again, it's the free thing.

Another thing you have to love is when some lady asks for a glass of water, four sugar packets, and seven lemon wedges.

"No, I don't want a drink. This will do just fine."

What she means is, "I don't want to *pay* for a drink. I'll just take all your stuff and make some free lemonade."

A quick heads up, sugar and lemons cost money, too.

There's another thing I should tell you about. This is something that no one in the restaurant wants you to know, but there are a lot of people out there who have figured it out. The big secret is, if you complain about things, you will get stuff for free.

Now, don't get me wrong, if there is a problem with any part of your meal, you have every right to complain about it. You should be able to get whatever you want, however you want it, and, if it isn't right, the restaurant should not only fix it, but compensate you for any inconvenience.

This is the way it works in most every restaurant, as well it should.

The problem with this is there are quite a few eggheads out there who have figured this out, and they use this to get free crap. People who do this are dirtbags. They are the lowest of the low. They are the slime that oozes out of scum.

I have seen people devour their meal, leaving nothing more than a morsel of meat on their plate, then begin bitching to high heaven that it was the worst, most overcooked, flavorless thing they have ever put in their mouth.

Then why did you eat it? If you would have said something earlier I could have had everything done right.

The thing is, these people are not interested in getting it fixed. They're interested in getting it free.

It is the free thing in its most ugly form. You might as well put on a neck brace and say you got whiplash from chewing your steak.

The Big Digs hotel is a major chain and they take their customer service seriously. At the hotel, we live and die by our customer satisfaction scores. It is the easiest place on the planet to get free stuff.

Many of our guests get free stuff without even trying. We give away so much, I sometimes wonder how we turn a profit.

Here's an example: It's a summer night and I'm working the bar with one of the She Devils. She is waiting on a woman and her three children out on the back patio. After dinner, the woman decides she'd like to have a glass of wine. At our bar, we offer two sizes. You have your choice between a 6-ounce or 9-ounce glass. The woman decides she would like the 9-ounce glass.

Jokingly, her server says, "Go big or go home, right?"

Now this might seem like an innocent enough comment. Most people would take it in the spirit it was intended, have a little chuckle, and get on with their life. Not this lady. I can only assume she had lived under a rock and, therefore, had never heard the expression. She went to the front desk and complained that her server told her to go home.

Our management comped her entire meal. That means she got the whole thing free.

Basically, she got $90 of free food and drinks because she didn't get the joke. Pretty sweet, huh?

Not only that, two managers took this particular She Devil into the back room and gave her a twenty-minute lecture on making inappropriate comments to her guests. I guess they didn't get the joke, either.

Out back of the Big Digs hotel, which is oceanfront, we have an elaborate pool area. There are two huge swimming pools, an open-air cafe, dozens of recliners, some hammocks, and a few cabanas. It's a really nice set up.

A friend of mine who lives locally asked me if I could get her some passes so she could bring her kids up and hang out at the pool, as the area is reserved for hotel guests. I told her, "There are no passes. Just show up."

"But what if I get caught?" she asked.

"Don't worry about it," I told her. "If anyone with a name tag approaches you, just start complaining about your room or tell them you had breakfast in the restaurant and your eggs were runny. They will probably buy you a bottle of champagne."

I don't know if she ever tried it.

The whole free thing is part of the business. People get free stuff without even trying. Others make it their mission to get all the free stuff they can.

There are no words to express how much it sucks when a five-top finishes their entire meal and that one guy complains because his potatoes were cold and now thinks the entire bill should be taken care of. I've seen it happen, over and over again.

You want me to comp your $175 bill because you didn't like the potatoes? Can't I just get you some fresh potatoes?

I understand it. I hate it and it drives me crazy, but I most certainly understand it.

Everybody loves getting stuff for free. There would be something wrong with you if you didn't.

Free food.

Free booze.

Free love.

Free for all.

Free basing.

All you can eat.

Open bar.

Buy one get one half off.

Buy one get one free.

For a limited time only.

A round of waters for the table.

An extra side of ranch.

One more loaf of bread.

A bottomless cup of Coca-Cola.

Go big or go home, right?

It's the world we live in. It's a part of who we are. It's out there for the taking and we might as well get our share of the pie before somebody else comes along and snatches it away. Why shouldn't we?

It's our money and as long as we're spending it, we're going to get everything we can and we're going to act any way we want while we're getting it. Screw everybody else.

All this talk is actually making me kind of hungry. I think I'll go to happy hour and grab a little snack.

Of course, I'll get there an hour early and maybe I'll ask for some crackers and water while I'm waiting. I think I'll get a side of ranch dressing, too.

You know what? Just for kicks, I think I'll complain the crackers are stale and the water isn't cold enough. Why not?

CHAPTER FIVE
YOU CREATE A DIVERSION AND I'LL MAKE A RUN FOR IT

So, are you ready to quit your job and join the restaurant business yet? I mean, I am painting a truly lovely vision of what it's like to work in this biz.

I need to tell you about a reoccurring dream I have. I am working at the Freedom Steakhouse and Brewery with a friend of mine. We are the only two people working this particular day, and the restaurant suddenly gets hit with a big rush. The thing is, in my dream, the Freedom Steakhouse and Brewery is always much bigger than it is in real life and it actually seats 450. Sometimes, in this dream, my section stretches out for miles and is packed with people.

I spend the entire dream running around in a frenzy, trying to get everyone taken care of, but I can never quite catch up. All of the people in my section are getting angrier and angrier and, before I know it, I am completely buried and have no idea what I'm supposed to be doing. I sometimes wake up in a cold sweat after.

It's worth mentioning that I haven't worked at the Freedom

Steakhouse and Brewery in years, but I still have the dream from time to time.

In the dream, it's like taking the worst case of weeds I've ever been in and multiplying it by a thousand.

I don't think people outside of the business understand how frustrating and difficult this job can be at times. When it hits the fan, it hits it hard. It's more like the shit storm hitting the windmill.

When the restaurant goes on a two-hour wait (which is very common in the summer) it ripples throughout the restaurant and affects every person who works there. It's like running in waist-deep water. It's like chasing your own tail.

First off, there is nothing like waiting two hours to eat to put people in a pleasant mood (I am being sarcastic). So now you cram about 550 people into our place and it's about 140 degrees and most everyone is on the verge of snapping at any moment (both customers and servers). This is when you find out what people are made of. This is where you separate the men from the boys (or the women from the girls). This is crunch time.

I'm not sure I can adequately describe what this feels like.

You are probably thinking, "So what? I've been busy at my job, too. What's the big deal?"

Unless you have run back and forth for six straight hours, nonstop, and kept track of 45 things at once, with angry people staring you down and angrier people bitching you out, you might not know what I'm talking about. This is the world we live in.

Let me try to explain.

Your shift starts at four. The place is packed when you walk in the door and the management has no choice but to throw you to the wolves. You have a five-table section and four of them are seated. Three of them have nothing in front of them and have not been greeted. One has plates and drinks.

You have no idea who got there first so you pick one of them at random and you approach them with a smile. It's a six-top and they are not happy. The first thing they want to do is bitch to you about how long they have been waiting (which they always exaggerate by at least twenty minutes).

You politely smile and nod while they continue to complain. Meanwhile, you are glancing around at the other tables in your section. All of them are staring back at you with angry looks on their faces.

All you can do is apologize for the wait they've experienced and explain that you just walked in the door. You assure them that now that you are here, you will make sure they are taken care of.

Still bitching and moaning, they give you their drink order. One dumbass decides to order his dinner, but you explain that you're going to get the drinks and you will be back to take his order.

Next, you swing by the elderly two-top who have been patiently waiting. You completely misread these people and they are not at all angry. In fact, they are the two sweetest people you have ever met. The woman thinks you remind her of her grandson and she wants to tell you all about him, but you would just like to get her drink order and be on your way.

The number three table that you haven't been to yet is glaring back at you and there is no mistaking their mood. They are pissed and one guy is waving his arms, back and forth, like he's in a lifeboat and trying to signal the rescue plane, but you are having trouble getting away from the sweet couple without being rude.

Finally, you get their drink order and you swing by table number three, a four-top. They want to complain about the wait as well. It turns out that they were seated before any of the other tables and they aren't happy that you visited the other two tables first. You try to explain the situation, but they are beyond consoling. These people have decided their experience is going to suck and they're going to be a problem all night.

You finally get past the bitching and you begin taking their drink order. As you are doing this, the one table that had drinks and plates in front of them and seemed fine gets up and leaves. At the same time, your open table is seated a three-top.

You finish taking the drink order and you swing by the three-top to tell them you will be right with them, and you go back to the bar to make your twelve drinks. Chances are two of these drinks will be frozen drinks and will roughly double your labor time.

You come back to your tables with a tray full of drinks and you go through the dinner specials as you drop them off. Everyone is ready to order but you explain that you will be right back to take their food orders.

To your horror, another four-top has seated itself at the dirty table that just left.

You drop off all your drinks, blowing off the sweet couple as politely as you can, because she still wants to tell you about her grandson, and you run by the three-top for a drink order.

From there you go by the dirty table. There are no bus boys working in the bar, so you grab as many dirty plates as you can carry while you take their drink order.

After making seven more drinks, you drop them off and bus the rest of the dirty table. Tables one and three are ready to place their dinner orders and table two still wants to talk. At least three people at your five tables are ready for refills on their drinks.

You take the dinner orders at tables one and three, drop off the refills, and now you take the dinner order of the sweet couple at table two. Tables four and five are still looking at menus and you know you have an extra couple of minutes, so you even chat with the sweet couple for a bit, but you're careful not to get too caught up in anything you can't get away from.

From there, it's off to the kitchen to make salads and bread. You get tables one and three started before going back to tables four and five for dinner orders. You put in the dinners and go to get salads for the sweet old couple, along with refills for six people throughout your section. Once table two's salads are out, you make another check on drinks before getting salads for four and five.

By this time, table one has their food and table three will be right behind them. You check on one. They need ranch dressing, extra bread, and some kind of lemon pepper sauce you don't usually carry and will have to be made special. By the time you are done with this, three has their food, two and five need drinks, and four has decided they want to change their dinner order, even though you have already rung it in.

Your night has just started and this is pretty much the way it will go for the next five and a half hours. You have barely been at work for half an hour.

It sounds pretty awful, doesn't it? It can be.

Now, I'm going to tell you something completely crazy. It's something I don't quite understand myself. It's something that defies all logic.

When things are totally manic and out of control, there is a calm that comes over you. It's like an athlete hitting the zone. Everything comes together and the impossible becomes commonplace. You let go of the anxiety and something else takes over. It becomes like choreography. The restaurant is like some kind of insane ballet with each server and staff member playing their imperfect parts to perfection. It's kind of a zen thing. Of course, zen is all about ying and yang and, when the bottom falls out, there is no worse place on earth, but when things are going smooth, it is something to see.

When it's all over, you feel like you were hit by a truck. Every muscle in your body aches, your knees are throbbing, and you can barely stand on your feet, but there is a certain satisfaction in knowing you kicked some serious ass.

I will tell you another crazy thing. You would think when things are going haywire and the restaurant is at its most insane is usually when you would make the most mistakes. It's not the case, at all.

It's the slow times that kill you. It's when you have three tables, the night is dragging, and you're bored to tears when you start screwing up. I don't know why this is, but it always seems to be the way it works out.

What can I say? This is a crazy business.

It's also a job a lot of people can't do. At least, a lot of people can't do it well.

Many times, the people who can't do it well rarely have a clue as to how inept they really are. These people usually think they are out there kicking ass along with everyone else. It's the people working around them and the people sitting in their sections who see it. Working beside a weak link sucks. It usually means you will have to work twice as hard as normal to keep yourself out of the weeds.

Now, of course, everyone can have an off day. None of us are perfect and everyone makes mistakes. That isn't what I'm talking about. I'm referring to the people who just do not possess the mental facilities or physical skills to do what I do.

I think I mentioned earlier how this isn't brain surgery and I'm not likening it to anything close. It takes another kind of intelligence to be good at this job. It's probably more of a common sense thing, an ability to adapt. It's the capacity to organize and manage the things around you, to keep your head when things go ballistic.

Some people lose their minds when things go crazy in a busy restaurant. They can't focus on the things they need to get done and they end up drowning in their own inadequacies. This is a pitiful sight to witness. It is sad to see a fellow human being reduced to a lump of useless confusion on the verge of tears.

You probably think I am exaggerating. I wish I was.

These people can put themselves in the weeds on even a slow night. They panic over the slightest thing and work themselves into a frenzy over nothing. These are the people who melt down when the going gets tough.

The thing is, when you see this happening around you, you're usually much too busy to show any kind of sympathy or compassion for these people. Their incompetence puts a strain on everyone around them, making everyone's job harder than it needs to be.

This is when you see people who are normally very sweet and considerate say things like, "Get the hell out of my way," or, "Do you think you could bus your damn table?"

This does not make them bad people. They are just too weeded for civility. In most other situations, these people would be very nice to the person in question.

Sometimes the people who aren't very good at this do not have the physical ability to do the job. Their body just doesn't possess the extra gear needed to work at this pace.

While everyone else is running at full speed, you can spot these people shuffling back and forth, at a leisurely pace, as though they have nothing in particular to do.

Sometimes, it isn't a physical deficiency holding people back. Sometimes it is a choice, and these people are the very worst to work with. I'm talking about the lazy slackers with no work ethic, the people who are perfectly content letting others do the hard work while they coast by, doing just enough to get by.

With the people who try, you tend to cut them some slack when possible. Most of us will go out of our way to help them out when we can. The people who don't try, not so much. They are a drain on everyone around them. When the you-know-what is hitting the fan, these are the people who drag the rest of us down with them, putting us all in the weeds. They are lazy pieces of garbage, spoiled ass-wipes who are used to relying on Mommy and Daddy to provide everything they need to survive.

What can I say? Some people are afraid of hard work. They avoid it at all costs. These are the people who spend two hours getting out of doing something that would take five minutes to get done.

These are the bartenders who spend half an hour talking to one customer, never bothering to look around them while their coworkers are running around like maniacs. These are the servers who are off in the dish room, gossiping with the girls while their coworker is getting flagged down by *their* table every two minutes because they are out of ranch dressing and haven't seen their server since Nixon was in office. This is the bartender who is busy stocking glasses while I'm having my ass handed to me.

It's no fun. I have no use for these people and I can tell you, from experience, no one else in the restaurant does, either.

Fortunately, these people usually end up filtering themselves out of the restaurant, eventually. Even the keen, eagle-eye of management will, sooner or later, begin to realize who the weak links on their staff are. This usually occurs after months of complaining by the person's coworkers, dozens of comped checks for dissatisfied customers, and a few piercing Yelp reviews.

Speaking of Yelp reviews. I'm all for Yelp, Open Table, and all the other restaurant review sites out there. By all means, if you have a great experience at a bar or restaurant, it is wonderful that you want to spread the word. If you have a truly dreadful experience, you have every right to post it as well, possibly saving some other poor soul a similar fate.

But if your dining experience was overall pleasant, except for the fact your medium steak came out medium rare, is it really necessary to sabotage the reputation of the business with a scathing review? Can we keep things in perspective? Just because you have been entrusted with the almighty power of passing judgment on your chicken salad sandwich doesn't mean you need to nit-pick every detail until it sounds like you had dinner at a third-world labor camp.

Legitimate complaints? Bring 'em on. But there is no need to drive a thriving business into bankruptcy because your fries came out cold.

Okay, back to server talk.

Another sub genre of restaurant employee is one I like to call the ditz. We have all been around these people. These are the people who just don't have a clue. These are the ones who, when you ask them a question, stare back at you like you're speaking Japanese.

I should preface this by saying, we all have our ditzy moments from time to time, but others take it to another level.

Being a ditz doesn't necessarily make you a bad person. It doesn't even make you a bad server or bartender. In fact, at times, the ditzes can be a lot of fun. They can even make your whole night.

Let me give some examples of things I have seen these people do.

At the bar I worked, we had a system we used when ordering food. We would name your tab after the approximate place you were sitting at the bar. So, if you are sitting by the pole we named your tab "pole." If you are sitting by the beer taps, you might be named "taps." This was our system for keeping things straight and lots of bars do something similar.

One day some guy was sitting in front of the ice bin (this is a bin filled with ice) and the bartender named the tab "ice bin." The guy ordered chicken wings. When they were done, a young girl was given the task of running the food out to him. She read the name on the tab and proceeded to take the wings to the storage area of the kitchen and set it on top of the ice machine (this is a machine that makes ice). The only time anyone goes back there is when he or she is in need of something. There are certainly never any customers back there eating.

At the Freedom Steakhouse and Brewery, one of the desserts we offered was a fudge brownie sundae. This was a hot brownie topped with vanilla ice cream and chocolate syrup. If I ever waited on you back in the day, there is a very good chance you have never heard of this dessert as it is an incredible pain in the ass to make and I sometimes conveniently forgot to mention it when you asked about desserts.

One of the new people at our restaurant needed to make one of these desserts and asked one of the other servers, "How can I heat the brownie without melting the ice cream?"

Surely I don't need to explain to you that the ice cream is added *after* the brownie is heated, do I?

This might have been the same girl who locked herself in the employee's bathroom, which locks from the inside, and banged on the door for twenty minutes to get someone to let her out.

Rest assured, if you do anything stupid while working in a restaurant, it will be the main topic of conversation that night when everyone gets off work and is having a cocktail. It is just too much fun.

Okay, this next one I feel a little bit guilty about telling. It concerns a girl I used to work with. I will begin by saying she was a very sweet young girl, but a tad on the naive side.

The Freedom Steakhouse and Brewery had a sister restaurant a few miles away. Our old GM used to make various bets with the GM of the other restaurant from time to time.

On one extremely slow day, our GM bet $50 that he could get one of his employees to do something truly goofy. He picked this girl to run up to the other store because he told her we were all out of steam for the kitchen and we needed to borrow two cans. Again, I should hope I don't have to explain that steam does not come in cans (everyone knows you can only buy it in cartons).

This poor girl drove all the way up to the other restaurant, where their GM had taken two jumbo cans of tomato paste, ripped off the labels and wrote *Steam* in black magic marker. She retrieved the cans and brought them back to our restaurant, to everyone's delight and to her horror when she found out what was going on.

To our GM's credit, he gave the girl the fifty bucks. It was the least he could do after humiliating her. I would never do anything like that to someone. (Don't worry, Lauren, I won't use your name.)

Another good one was to send the new girl to clean the coffee machine, telling her to be sure to empty the water out of it first. The coffee machine has its own water line and never runs out of water. Some of them will work at it for an hour before they figure it out.

Earlier, I was telling you about how hard my job can be. This would be a good time to tell you about the worst shift I ever worked.

It was years ago and Hurricane Charley had just blown through Myrtle Beach. As far as hurricanes go, it wasn't too bad and the damage was minimal. It hit us overnight and by noon or so, the next day, it was gone and the sun was shining.

I went into work that afternoon and the power was still out, as some of the power lines in town were down. We all sat around the bar, waiting to see what would happen. Our GM was waiting to see if the power was going to come on.

Around four or so, it looked like it wasn't going to happen so he let a bunch of the people go home. Some of us (the stupid ones) hung around a little longer, just for the hell of it. I think we thought it might become some sort of impromptu party.

Just as we were about to call it quits, the power popped back on and our GM decided to go ahead and open with a skeleton crew. How busy could we possibly get?

As I've told you, the Freedom Steakhouse and Brewery was located in a large tourist complex. For the sake of this book, and because it is still there, we will call the complex Broadway at the Sand by the Ocean. Apparently, unbeknownst to us, we were the only restaurant in the complex to open back up that evening.

By five o'clock we were packed to capacity. There were a few problems, though. One was the kitchen wasn't ready. Nothing was prepped and the grills needed time to heat up. It would be another hour before we could start serving food. The other problem was the computer system had gone down and the only computer that was working was all the way in the back of the restaurant (about as far away from the bar as you can get).

In the bar alone, we were running with five people. One behind the bar, two on the floor, and two in the beer garden. On a busy night, we normally run with nine people.

A friend of mine (named Brian) and I had the beer garden.

By the time the kitchen was up, people were getting nasty. They were pissed because they hadn't been able to find anything open, they were pissed because they had to wait to order, and they were pissed because they weren't getting the attention they wanted. How much of this was my fault?

We continued to explain to people how we had just been through a hurricane and were short-handed. To be perfectly honest, most people were very understanding. The ones who weren't were pretty bad. Again, it's that whole squeaky wheel thing.

So, this is how the night went. You would go out and get as many orders as you could, before going in and making all your drinks. After you dropped them off, you would run down to the other side of the restaurant and stand in line, with all the other servers and bartenders, to use the one working computer.

Once you had rung everything in, you would run back out to your section, where pretty much everyone needed something else and was angry because they couldn't find you. You would also have to help out with making salads and what not for the girl behind the bar, because she was swamped and unable to get away.

It was, pretty much, my nightmare come to life.

At one point, I was waiting in line for the computer and I looked up to find Brian waiting behind me. Brian had been under the assumption that we weren't going to open and he'd been out having a few cocktails before coming in. He was sweating like I have never seen another human being sweat before. He looked up at me and said, "This might be the night that I just walk out. This is bullshit."

I answered, "When you leave, I'm going to be right behind you, because I'm not doing this shit by myself."

Neither of us walked out. We finished the shift and I think we all made a little over two hundred bucks each. Not much considering how hard we worked.

It was a night that I got a complaint, too. One of my tables had two young couples sitting at it. I'm guessing they were in their early twenties. They had dinner and afterward they asked me to separate their checks for them. Normally this would not be a problem. I explained how we had just been through a hurricane, were short-staffed, and how I didn't have time to do it with our malfunctioning computer situation. I also explained that everything on their check was itemized and all they needed to do was go through and add up what they had to get their totals.

"But we have credit cards."

I explained how this would not be a problem and that, when they handed me their cards, they could tell me how much they wanted me to put on it. This is not something I would normally do, but I was still weeded with my other tables and barely had time to think. I guess they didn't know how to add. Instead, they went to a manager and complained because I refused to split their checks.

If you are a young couple who was vacationing in Myrtle Beach the week of Hurricane Charley and you ate at the Freedom Steakhouse and Brewery and asked for separate checks and your server said he didn't have time and you complained to a manager and you are reading this now ... I hate your guts. You are ignorant scum and I hope there is a hurricane every time you vacation in Myrtle Beach.

It was by far the hardest shift I've ever worked and one of the worst nights of my life. The five of us finished the night with shots of So-Co Kamikazes (Southern Comfort) before we went out for cocktails and to talk about how hard our night was.

Of course, this night was the exception to the rule and usually it is nowhere close to that bad. I'm also sure that every business has its horror stories. It just seems to me that our business can be particularly brutal at times.

Once, I was out running some errands and I decided to stop at a Denny's for lunch. I think I had a craving for an omelet. While sitting at the counter, I overheard two of Denny's veteran waitresses talking to a young girl who appeared to be in training.

They were discussing the rigors of serving at Denny's and both confessed that they had actually broken down into tears during their first shifts. The stress had just been too much for them. They assured the newbie, that if this happened to her, it would be quite normal and she should not be alarmed. That says a lot about what we do.

Even at Denny's.

I have to say, I have never actually burst out crying at work. I do, sometimes, like to get to work early and have a good cry before going in, though. I find it very cleansing.

That said, as bad as it can get, there is one thing we all hate more. It's boredom. The dry spells can make you crazy, and there is no boredom quite like restaurant boredom.

In a beach town, like Myrtle Beach, the winters can be particularly brutal.

Like I told you, the Freedom Steakhouse and Brewery was a very popular spot, with the busiest happy hour in all of Myrtle Beach. Even in the winters we maintained a steady crowd and always had a core of local regulars who kept us going through the slim times. Not everyone in Myrtle Beach is as lucky. When I worked at the Crustacean House, there were winter nights that I walked out of there with less than ten bucks after a seven-hour shift.

Bar boredom can be excruciating. It's like listening to paint dry. I have seen people do some crazy stuff to pass the time.

I remember playing football in the bar at Hull Street Blues on a particularly slow Sunday night. Not too long ago a bunch of guys were playing football in the dining room at the Freedom Steakhouse and Brewery, too. I didn't get in on the game but it brought back some old memories. The night we played in Hull Street we took out a table, but nobody got hurt.

To pass the time we come up with all sorts of games. Trivia is big and we sometimes break off into teams to compete in the various versions we come up with. "Name That Tune" was very popular, but the satellite radio station we listen to tends to play the same songs every night and it gets stale pretty quick. Crossword puzzles and word games are a staple in any bar or restaurant.

One day back at Freedom, our GM and a few of the bartenders were out back of the restaurant with their golf clubs hitting balls out into the complex's lake. I think they were betting on distance and accuracy.

Our GM also had a remote control boat he would take out sometimes, but the damn thing kept dying in the middle of the lake. He would have to wait for the tide to take it to the shallows where he could retrieve it.

Speaking of that lake, someday they are going to drag that thing and they are going to find some amazing stuff lying on the bottom. When I worked at the Crustacean House, there was a large deck out back for dining outside. With a lot of servers, it was common practice to dump dirty plates, glasses and silverware off the back deck rather than take the time to carry it back to the kitchen. There must be thousands of dishes, forks, and knives out there.

I also have firsthand knowledge of water heaters, stoves, and other pieces of restaurant equipment finding its way into the lake. Sometimes it got there because it was easier than having it hauled off and sometimes it was just because people were bored and had nothing better to amuse themselves.

99 bottles of beer on the wall.

99 bottles of beer.

Take one down and pass it around.

98 bottles of beer on the wall.

Imagine being in a quiet room and doing that all night. That's kind of what bartending on a slow night is like. Only without the cool music.

It must be a lot like working in a coal mine, but I have never actually worked in a coal mine so I'm only guessing on this point. For all I know, coal mining might be fun and engaging work.

These are the nights where it's kind of dangerous to tend bar. These are the nights where you are one stupid customer away from going totally postal.

This leads us to another topic. This topic is burnout. Burnout hits everyone who works in the industry at one time or another. This is just a natural fact. When you deal with the public on such a one-on-one basis, this is an inevitable consequence.

Burnout occurs after long stints in this business. Some people are overcome with burnout and it turns them away from the biz. They are forced to find another way to make a living. Others are overcome with burnout and they are transformed into the ultimate anti-people person. They hate everything about what we do, and any contact with other human beings becomes pure torture. At this point, they are merely going through the motions, trying to get through every shift without ripping someone's head off. These people are complete assholes to everyone around them, including the people they work with. I'm sure we have all seen people in many professions who suffer from varying degrees of this. You have to feel sorry for anyone who has it this bad.

With still others, burnout occurs every once in a while and consumes them for brief periods of time. During these times, they feel like they cannot do this for another day without harming themselves or others. These people have to battle through these periods before things return to normal. I fall into this latter category.

I can't tell you how bad these times suck. It's rough getting through your day when things are like this. Especially when you consider that you have to remain in a good mood and treat everyone with kindness and respect when all you really want to do is slap them upside the head.

For me, these spells usually don't last too long, and as long as I remain quiet and subdued, I can get through them without incident. Once they are over, everything returns to normal and I can continue my work as usual.

This might be a good time to let you in on one of the darkest and well-kept secrets concerning the service industry. This is the thing of which we do not speak and there is a very good chance I will be kicked out of the bartenders union for mentioning it. As long as I'm giving you a truthful look at the business, I might as well throw it out there. It's time to air out our dirty laundry once and for all.

In this job, as I told you earlier, you are constantly on your feet. You spend the better part of your shift running back and forth and there is seldom a chance to slow down or sit down (especially in the summer).

All of this running around can lead to other uncomfortable problems to contend with.

I am referring to, of course, what some people call Swamp Ass. Others call it Crotch Rot, and still others simply refer to it as Sweating in the Nether Regions.

This can be an incredible pain in the ass (literally), and when you factor in the various parts for rubbing, friction, and eventual chafing, you can see what a problem this can be. If you are being waited on by someone who is very busy and it's during one of the hot summer months, there is a very good chance this person is suffering from this infliction.

The only known cure for this is a liberal dose of corn starch, and it is why you will almost always find a box in the employee bathroom of every major restaurant across the country. I even know of one restaurant that kept a box in the walk-in cooler for the cooling effect.

Hey boss, Henry's got his pants down in the cooler again!

What you need to understand about this practice is that everyone who uses the box is on the honor system and no double dipping is allowed. If that doesn't make you close to your coworkers, I don't know what will.

I should point out that corn starch, although it does help, does not eliminate this condition completely. Even after applying your CS to the afflicted area, after hours of running around in the summer heat, it will still feel like you are baking bread in your underpants.

Of course, I, personally, have never had much of a problem with this condition and I have never indulged in this tradition. Even if I had, I would never admit to it in writing.

Here's another secret about bartending nobody outside the business wants you to know about. This one is an absolute that applies to everyone who has worked in this business over the last thirty years.

When someone orders a Piña Colada and you are in the process of making it, you must *ALWAYS*, 100 percent of the time, sing *The Piña Colada Song* in your head.

If you like Piña Coladas

And getting caught in the rain...

Every bartender I have ever talked to about this has given me the same answer to this question. The act of making this drink automatically triggers this reaction inside all of our heads. It does not even matter if you like the song or not. It just happens.

Speaking of frozen drinks, we all hate to make them, and they are a surefire way to put you in the weeds. Unless you happen to work at a daiquiri bar, this is another absolute truth and I suspect it's probably true there, too. They are a royal pain in the ass, and when you order one your bartender is cringing on the inside.

I will let you in on another secret. When you order said frozen drink, you are getting little to no alcohol in that drink. I can pretty much guarantee your bartender is stiffing you on your drink. It's his or her revenge factor for making them go to all the trouble of making a strawberry daiquiri when they are in the weeds. I've even seen bartenders pour a bit of rum down the inside of the straw, so that first sip tastes like you are getting a strong drink and not the virgin daiquiri you are actually drinking.

I, of course, have never done such a thing.

There used to be a bar in Baltimore that kept a blender nailed, upside down, to the ceiling behind the bar. When someone ordered a frozen drink, the bartender would simply point to the ceiling and say, "Sorry, I can't reach the blender."

I always wanted to work at that bar.

Speaking of rum drinks, here's another bar secret. All of those fancy fruit drinks you love so much, they are all pretty much the same thing. Rum and fruit juice.

I don't care if you order a Bahama Mama, a Rum Runner, or a Mai Tai. In most of the bars I know, you are getting rum and fruit juice. They throw some grenadine in it to make it red.

This may not always be the case. There are bars that specialize in these types of drinks and follow the recipes very closely. There are even dedicated bartenders who follow drink recipes to the letter, but these are usually newbies who haven't realized that nobody can tell the difference anyway.

Here's another secret. If you walk into a restaurant within 45 minutes of closing time and order a cup of coffee, you are drinking decaf. Chances are, in an effort to get a jump on closing duties, your server has already dumped the regular and cleaned the coffee machine, leaving only a half a pot of decaf. I've even seen people add hot water to the last of the decaf in an effort to stretch it out and avoid dirtying another pot.

While we're on secrets, here's one that seems pretty obvious to me. If you walk into a restaurant minutes before they close and sit down for dinner, everyone in that building hates your guts. They would much rather waterboard you than take your dinner order. They have spent the whole night getting their butts kicked and have just finished cleaning and resetting their section. They were minutes from walking out the door and have plans to meet some friends for a drink.

When you and your family settle in for a four-course meal two minutes before closing time, it is like a punch in the stomach. Back in the kitchen, the cooks are throwing things around and cussing like sailors. Even the Mexican dishwasher, who doesn't speak English, is spouting off some choice American curse words.

When the manager seats you and says, "Yes, of course we are

open. Please have a seat," he is biting his lip, trying to hold back his true feelings.

Sorry, that's just the way it is.

I mentioned in one of the earlier chapters, how I've never witnessed anyone messing with a customer's food. I never have, but if it were going to happen, this would be the time. You might want to get to that restaurant a little earlier next time.

So, there you have it. Everything you need to know about what it's like to work in the restaurant industry in a nutshell. If you weren't ready to quit your day job before and join the ranks of the service industry, you have to be by now.

CHAPTER SIX
WALLOWING IN YOUR OWN FILTH

I'm going to tell you something that's going to be difficult to wrap your mind around. It's something you probably don't know unless you've experienced it first hand.

People are pigs.

I don't mean like messy or untidy. I'm talking filthy, disease-ridden, bug-infested pigs.

Trust me, with most people, you would not want to eat or drink after them, touch anything they've touched, or even be in the same room as them. When they are feeding, you can magnify these qualities by a hundred.

I will tell you something else, too. Scabies are real and lots of people have them. Not only scabies, but all sorts of other infectious manifestations, ailments, and all around disorders.

Now, I'm not referring to actual health issues such as sicknesses or diseases or anything in that realm. I certainly wouldn't wish any such thing on anyone and I feel for anyone who has to endure anything like that.

I'm talking about the self-inflicted kinds of things. The things that stem from bad grooming, a total disregard for cleanliness, and poor table manners.

Okay, there's no law that says you have to smell good in public. I realize that, but why would you want to leave the house smelling like fertilizer and old cheese? Do you think nobody is going to notice?

I guarantee if you are one of these people, everyone in the restaurant is talking about you while you eat.

Did you get a whiff of the guy at table 99?

Here's a good rule of thumb. Before you go out for the evening, sit in your car, roll up the windows, and take a deep breath. If you detect the scent of something that reminds you of unwashed feet, go wash your stinky ass.

In this day and age, there is no excuse to smell like you live at the dog pound. There are a whole assortment of soaps, colognes, and deodorants available out there. Take your pick. If you need a combination of two or three of these to cover your stench, then by all means, make the investment. It will pay off in the long run.

We had one guy who came into our restaurant all the time. He was actually a pretty nice guy, but he talked constantly about nothing in particular and he smelled like rotting vegetables.

It was my idea to do a reality show where contestants are placed alone on a deserted island with this guy and a gun with one bullet. The idea was to see how long it would take for contestants to shoot either themselves or this guy. If it were me, I think I'd shoot myself. There is always the chance you could miss when aiming at someone else. I wanted to call my show "Stinky Island."

I realize there may be people out there with genetic or glandular disorders which may cause this condition, but my guess is these people are few and far between and that most of this stems from poor personal hygiene. Just wash your funky butt every once in a while. How hard is that? I don't want to smell you when I approach your table.

If you are the husband, wife, boyfriend, or girlfriend of someone who smells like meat that was left out in the sun for three days, how about doing us all a favor and drop some subtle hints?

Do you want to jump in the shower before we go out?

Why don't you try that cologne I got you for Christmas?

Do you smell rotten eggs?

I'm not saying you have to hurt their feelings. Be tactful. Leave a bottle of Old Spice next to their cereal bowl in the morning. Go to bed with a clothespin on your nose.

Do they even still make clothespins?

Don't go thinking that covering your odor is going to completely solve the problem, either. For one thing, colognes can only cloak so much, and the only real cure is good old-fashioned soap and water. Besides, you don't want to be that guy who smells like he bathed in Hi Karate.

These people are fairly easy to pick out in a crowd, as there are usually not many people standing close to them. These are the ones where you approach their table and your eyes start to burn. By the time you get their dinner order, you feel like you were maced.

There is nothing wrong with throwing on a little smell-good, but let's not get carried away. If I can smell you from a block away, you might have overdone it a tad. If the people at your table are gagging and turning red, you might want to back down on the Musk for Men.

Here's another one. Why, after they wolf down a dozen spicy Buffalo wings, do people feel the need to get right in your face when they speak to you?

I am backing away because your breath could melt asphalt.

In this situation, I try to be as polite as possible. I turn my head slightly to the side or back off a tad. I might even bring my hand up over my face like I'm in serious contemplation over what you are telling me. The truth is, it smells like your tongue died in your mouth and I'm thinking of wearing a gas mask the next time I visit your table.

The cure to this dilemma is actually quite simple. Get out of my personal space. You do not need to be an inch from my face to tell me what kind of dressing you want on your salad. I can hear you from here. Unless you are getting ready to kiss me, and chances are that I don't want you to kiss me, you can back away a bit because your mouth smells like you're using it to store old seafood.

In fact, there is really no reason for you to invade my space at all. You do not need to touch me in any way. Keep your hands off my back, shoulder, arm, and ass. You do not need to take my hand in yours while telling me you need salt and pepper. I get it.

If you are a guy with the habit of constantly putting your hands on the female servers who wait on you, even though you do not know them at all, I can tell you that you are labeled a slime bucket and pervert. You are about one touch away from being labeled a sex offender and or stalker and chances are you are just creeping the girl out. You might be getting your jollies, but you are giving her the heebee jeebees.

No one is saying that we can't touch other people. Human contact is a very important part of life; just use your head. If you feel the need to touch a complete stranger who happens to bring you a vodka tonic, you're creepy. A handshake should be quite sufficient. Anything more than this is crossing the line. After a few times of seeing them you may even graduate to a quick hug or a pat on the shoulder, but you will need to feel them out on this and play it by ear.

Am I saying that I have never touched a woman I just met? Of course not, but in these situations there were usually some sort of signs given and there is a very good chance alcohol was involved and or money was exchanged. I'm just kidding about the money part. I haven't done that since I was a young man in the Army and I was in Puerto Rico and … actually, that's another story altogether.

The point is having respect for the people around you. This means not offending them with your odor as well as with your improper touches. This should go for everyone around you and not just the people serving you in bars and restaurants. Following these simple rules will most definitely improve the quality of your life. It will certainly improve the quality of everyone's around you.

I have been talking about how all of this relates to respecting others, but what about respecting yourself? You should want to be odor-free for yourself as much as for anyone else. This leads me to another subject. If this were a new chapter, I would call it, *What on Earth Were They Thinking When They Put that On?*

First off, anyone who knows me will never confuse me with any kind of fashion guru or expert. I am not a dedicated follower of fashion in any way. The fact is, I pay very little attention to fashion.

So, I'm not talking about girls who say things like, "Can you believe she wore those shoes with those pants?" or "That skirt is *so* last year." The women who work in the restaurant are busy doing that.

I wouldn't know the first thing about stuff like that. I'm strictly a jeans and T-shirt kind of guy. I'm talking about people who offend our eyes.

This is not an attack on big people. Some of my best friends are large people. Seventy percent of our country is overweight and it is quite common to be heavier than your recommended body weight. It's almost an American tradition.

This said, if you are five-foot-one and weigh in the area of 320, do you really need to wear the spandex pants? If you have a beer gut that makes it look like you are eight months pregnant and you are a guy, do you need to cut the shirt off at the belly? Speaking of which, if your shoulders and back are hairier than Sasquatch, let's leave the sleeves on, too.

If you are a large woman on the back of one of those rice burner motorcycles that you have to lean all the way forward on, let's forgo the thong bathing suit. It's just common courtesy.

Somebody call Wendy's! I think I just figured out where the beef is.

Okay, you're a big guy. Maybe you are even a real plumber. This does not mean you should be showing your ass crack at any time. Trust me. Pull up your dang drawers. Nobody thinks you're sexy.

Also, I know this is a beach town and seeing bathing suits during the summer is just every day life in Myrtle Beach, but here's a hint. I don't care what size you are, how good-looking you think you are, or how great shape you are in. Speedo bathing suits went out in the 1970s. No one thinks you look good in that thing. Everyone who sees you in it is making fun of you behind your back. And why is it that it's always the paunchy old guy wearing it with the gray body hair and the way-too-dark tan?

If your significant other enjoys seeing your jewels wrapped in a banana hammock, wait until you get back to the hotel room before parading around. The rest of us never did anything to you, and we don't deserve to be subjected to that.

By the way, ladies, pink hair is a young girl's game. If you are pushing sixty, it just looks disturbing.

Speaking of things you see at the beach, if you are 100 years old or if your wrinkled leathery skin looks 100 from years of lying out in the sun, by all means keep doing what you love doing. Soak up all the rays you want, but when you come off the beach and go out to dinner, put some damned clothes on. It's like seeing your grandmother in a bikini.

Here's another one that gets me. You are an elderly gentleman, enjoying a relaxing vacation on the beach. By all means, make yourself comfortable. Kick your shoes off, if you'd like, but please, for the love of God, get your nasty old man feet off the tabletop. People are trying to eat!

Another good rule to follow is *never* to wear your good dress shoes with your shorts or swimsuit. If you get to the beach and realize that you have left your tennis shoes or sandals back at home, DO NOT PUT ON YOUR PATENT LEATHER LOAFERS. This is never a good look.

Those shoes might look good with your Sunday-Go-To-Meeting Duds, but with your shorts or swimsuits they make you look like you went to school on the short bus. You are not impressing anyone, I don't care how nice those shoes are. Here's an idea. Go out and get yourself some flip-flops. You can get a pair at the beach for about two bucks and nobody will be making fun of you behind your back.

While we're on the subject, those sandals you bought are open for a reason. They are not made to be worn with black dress socks. If you do this, you are defeating the whole purpose. You might as well put your loafers back on.

If clowns had their own country, your picture would be on the money.

This isn't really a fashion thing but I've got another rule for you. It is NEVER okay to pick your nose in public. We had a guy who came into the Freedom Steakhouse and Brewery all the time. He could get his entire finger up his nose and he did it constantly. He thought nothing of it, like it wasn't out of the ordinary in the slightest and his finger pretty much remained in his nose for the entire time he sat at the bar.

When he left, we would put on rubber gloves and throw away everything he had touched.

While I'm on the subject, under no circumstance should you blow your nose and leave the nasty napkin or tissue out on the table for your server to pick up. Your mother probably doesn't work at my restaurant. If she did, she would be on hand to pick up after you. Since she is not, don't expect your server to do your dirty work. Do something with your snot rag.

Actually, with this one I'm going to let you in on another industry secret. If you work in a bar or restaurant for any amount of time, you will eventually lose your gag reflex completely. After a while, nothing will gross you out anymore. It is just something you sacrifice when deciding to become a bartender or server.

I personally am immune to all things groady and revolting. I have lost the ability to become nauseated by the sight of anything revolting.

Sure, maybe if I found a severed finger at a table, I might get a little queasy. Who am I kidding? I'd probably wrap it in a napkin and turn it in to the hostess stand. Now, a human head …

Hey, I watch people eat and drink for a living. Spend 45 minutes watching an insurance salesman from Indiana wolf down an open-faced roast beef sandwich with mashed potatoes. Those "Saw" movies got nothing on that.

In my defense, I should state that I have children so I've been over the vomit thing for years. For those of you who don't have kids, I will let you in on a little secret. You might think a good day is a night out with friends, dinner, and a movie, maybe a few drinks at your favorite watering hole. After you have children, a good day is any you don't have to touch poop. That's just the way it is.

I can tell you sincerely, in all my years in the business, I have seen every bodily fluid left behind at my bar. It isn't a pretty sight, but you become numb to it after a while. And guess who gets stuck cleaning it up?

You wouldn't believe the things that get left behind at tables. We ought to be issued haz-mat suits before clearing some of the things we have to clear. Dirty diapers, used tissues, dental floss, it all gets left behind. I have found food in every stage of chewedness. Sometimes it's even on a plate.

I suppose there was a time when I used to get grossed out over such things, but it's been so long I can barely remember. Nowadays, I grab the handiest and cleanest napkin within reach and scoop it onto a plate.

That pile of brown sludge that might have been meat or could be pudding? Piece of cake. I barely notice as I swipe into a pile with all the other leavings. I'll have it gone in a jiffy.

I could wait for the busboy to come along and take care of it, but chances are there's another five-top hovering over my shoulder and waiting to leave their own debris in my section. I just don't have the time to wait.

You do what you can. You try not to actually touch the offending items with your bare hands, but things happen. What are you going to do? You wash your hands with a Brillo pad and some lye soap and you're as good as new. I have touched things that would make a grown man shudder in fear. I'm not proud of it, but it comes with the territory.

My guess is that hand sanitizer was invented by a server. I have no proof of this and I'm too lazy to look it up so we'll go with it.

If you want to talk gross, we've barely touched on the eating habits of the North American restaurant patron.

Let me just start off by saying that no one is going to come by and take your plate before you are finished. There is no need to wolf down your food like you haven't eaten in a week.

Relax. Take your time. Enjoy your meal. It is not a race, there are no prizes given to the first one finished, and nobody wants to see you choke to death while trying to scarf down a meatball sub. Actually, that last part may or may not be true, depending on how you have treated your server to this point.

You are paying good money for that meal. Take the time to enjoy it.

It might be worth mentioning that I might be a little rusty on that whole Heimlich maneuver thing, so if you start choking on your pork chop, you might be on your own with that one.

The thing is that it is disgusting to watch someone shovel food into his face. Act like you've had a decent meal before.

Here's another one. Once the food is in your mouth, let's try to do everything we can to keep in there. I do not want to be bombarded with particles of chewed potato when I approach your table. In fact, once the food is in your mouth, I really don't want to see it again in any form. I certainly don't want to wear it.

There are a few simple steps that you can do to ensure that this does not happen.

1. Chew with your mouth closed. Didn't all of our parents teach us this when we were like five?

I once saw a beautiful young girl sitting at the bar and eating chicken wings and she was taking the largest most exaggerated chomps I have ever seen. It almost looked like she was unlocking her jaw between bites. Needless to say, she didn't seem all that attractive after watching this for ten minutes. To be honest, I still see that image when I close my eyes sometimes.

2. Do not attempt to speak with a mouthful of food. I've had people call me over in mid-chew to tell me they need a refill of sweet tea and the entire time I am wincing as bits of chicken are flying out of their mouth and hitting me about the head and shoulders. This is not a lot of fun.

Why don't you just go ahead and spit on me while you're at it?

If you need to convey an urgent message to me (such as you are low on iced tea) I will wait until you are done swallowing the wad of meatloaf you have stuffed into your pie hole. In the worst-case scenario, I will be right back.

If you feel your message to me is so important you can't wait the twenty seconds it will take to finish chewing, or the minute and a half it will take me to return, please do me the courtesy of holding your napkin over your mouth while you speak. Even your cupped hand will serve as an adequate barrier to protect me from the small pieces of dead animal and vegetation you are launching toward me with every word.

3. Sometimes when you are eating, you may be overcome with the involuntary urge to cough, sneeze, laugh, or one of the other things the human body can do without warning. This does not make you a bad person, but please make every possible attempt to do whatever you can to cover your mouth when this occurs. Your server and every person who has a plate or glass within striking range will appreciate this greatly.

Those are the big three when it comes to preventing your chewed food from ending up on or in someone else's person. I would hope nobody wants to be that guy, but you would be flabbergasted by how many people don't follow these simple rules.

Another thing to keep in mind when you are out in public is that you are *out in public.* This means that you are not in the privacy of your own home and you cannot act however you want.

This means that it is not okay to pick up your plate and lick it clean when you are done eating. What the hell is wrong with you?

How was the chow, Lassie?

Here's a hint. If you are out on a business luncheon with a perspective client and you pick up your plate and start licking it when you are done, you are not landing that account. That's just the way it works. I would say that in almost all of these cases the best bet is to keep your tongue in your mouth at all times. I get it. You liked the sauce. I'm glad you enjoyed it. That doesn't mean that you can resort back to the ways of primitive man. Soak it up with your bread. Scoop it up with your fork. Do not lick your plate under any circumstance.

Now that we've turned that stone over, how much food do you need to consume in one sitting?

Certainly, we are a country of over-indulgences, and eating too much is as common as blue eyes, but boy is it an ugly thing to witness firsthand. Do us all a favor and get a box to take that third dinner home with you.

Unless you are trying to get your money's worth at an all-you-can-eat restaurant or you're in training for one of those hot dog eating contests, there really is no good reason to stuff yourself like Jabba the Hut at a K&W Cafeteria. Chances are, a large portion of your meal has found its way to your face and chest along the way, anyway. You'd be better off taking it home where you can concentrate on cramming it all in there.

If I was a big boy who loved nothing more than gouging himself with as much food as my body could possibly handle, I think I would be a big fan of carry out, but that's just me.

Also, when out to eat, you should go to any length necessary to keep from making any sort of slurping, chomping, or loud chewing noises while eating. This is disgusting and it gives everyone around you the urge to slap you upside your ignorant head.

The best way to avoid this is to refer back to rule number one. If you are chewing with your mouth open, like a cow chewing its cud, there is a good chance there is an assortment of accompanying noises to go along with the visuals. There is also a good chance someone at your table is losing their appetite.

These are all things that make you a pig in everyone's eyes, but what about the things that affect only your server? What about the things you do that convince your server what a pig you are?

How about when someone breaks a glass? This is an innocent thing and everyone does it. I do it all the time and it's no big deal. Now, if you break that glass and I go and get the broom and dust pan, and when I go to clean it up, you can't even go to the trouble of moving your damned feet, then you are a friggin' pig. There is no way around it.

You broke the stupid thing. The very least you can do is get the hell out of my way.

This pretty much goes for anything I have to clean up. If you spill your drink, here's an idea … move your elbows so your server can clean it up. Get out of the way. Haven't you caused me enough grief to this point?

And by the way, if you call me over to your table to have me stand there while you and your old lady argue about whether or not you like your steak cooked medium or medium rare, you are a P.I.G. I have better things to do. Argue on your own time and call me over when you have decided. I'm not going anywhere. I will be around when you need me. There is no need to monopolize all of my time as I have other things to fetch for other people. If I'm in the mood for an argument, I will call my ex-wife.

In a similar vein, please do not call me over to watch you read the menu. When you have made your decision, by all means, call me over and I will be happy to take your order. When I am forced to stand there for three minutes while you casually read the menu from top to bottom, I am secretly fantasizing about sticking bamboo slivers under your fingernails.

Okay, maybe that one doesn't really make you a pig. That one makes you more of a jackass, but it's one of my personal pet peeves.

Another one.

If you have been nice and polite to me all through your meal and turn into an angry, raging jerk when I bring you your check you are not only a pig, you are an asshole to boot. You ordered the stuff and you ate the stuff, the prices are all listed on the menu. Why are you getting mad at me?

Did you think you were getting this meal for free?

Also, at the end of your meal, please do not give me the five-minute verbal tip in lieu of cash. These are the people who want to praise you for the great job you did, then turn around and stiff you on the tip. If you are planning to stiff me, just go ahead and leave. Your verbal tip is only wasting my time.

For the record, the verbal tip does me absolutely no good when I go to pay my electric bill. I know, because I've tried.

All right, you are a parent. Good for you. You're out to dinner and you want to teach your kid some social skills and tools they will need later in life. Teaching them to order their own drink or meal is a very good thing to do but after five minutes of listening to you say, "Tell the nice man what you want to drink," I can't decide which of you I dislike more. I've got nothing against your kid, but chances are I don't find him or her anywhere near as cute as you do. Just order the stupid milk for them and try again some other time. I would like to get back to my life.

While we are talking about kids, control your rug rats!

What is it with these people who let their children run wild in restaurants? I will let you in on another secret. It is not only the staff who hates you. Every person in the restaurant hates you and your bratty kids. I have enough adults to babysit during my shift. I do not need to take on the responsibility of being caregiver to your demon child. Not to mention, a busy restaurant is a dangerous place for small children to be running around unsupervised. When I am carrying a large tray of dinner plates, I probably can't see your 5-year-old scampering in front of me. Do us all a favor. Keep track of your brat. I don't want to hurt the little guy. It's only some of the parents I would like to hurt.

This one might not actually make you a pig, per say. Pigs look after their offspring better.

So, basically, you can see that you don't have to be a filthy, smelly, bug-infested scumbag to fall into the pig category. It's one way to get there but it's not the only way. There are all sorts of pigs out there and I wait on most of them at one time or another.

You have your dirty pigs, your rude pigs, your visually offensive pigs, and just your garden variety inconsiderate pigs. If you fall into one of these categories, I can only say, *suoeee, suoeee. Here piggy, piggy. It's feeding time. Come and get you some!*

CHAPTER SEVEN
SCREWED, BLUED, AND TATTOOED

It's a random Tuesday night and I'm working at the Big Digs Hotel. We're slammed. Because the restaurant was projected to have a slow night, management scheduled a skeleton crew and we are severely understaffed.

The place is packed. There is a butt in every seat, with more butts hovering around the taken tables, scavengers waiting to pounce the instant people get up. Actually, those latter people are more like buttholes.

You would think a convoy of buses pulled up out front, all of them full of angry and hungry people.

Two girls are working the floor and I'm alone behind the bar. I say that, but I'm barely behind the bar, at this point. I've picked up four tables on the floor, as well as my full bar. The girls have it worse than me.

Even though it's 22 degrees out, people have overflowed to the outside patio tables, demanding service in the frigid cold. As a result, the two She Devils probably have twelve tables each, half of them outside, where I can only imagine them shivering in their skimpy cocktail dresses while people in thick winter coats take their time deciding between the Brussels sprouts or broccolini with dinner.

There was no food runner scheduled, so the three of us, along with a manager, are taking turns running the food. This is especially fun because the kitchen is on the opposite side of the hotel, about as far away from the bar as you can get and still share a ZIP code.

My turn is up. When I get there, the kitchen is a zoo. Ticket times are approaching thirty minutes. The executive chef is yelling out food orders and plating sides, trying his best to keep things moving forward. There are three servers from the restaurant, along with the room service attendant, shouting out the various food items they need to fill orders. One lone manager is frantically working the expo line, scrounging through food tickets, trying to match up plates with orders. It's a lot like trying to find a haystack in a stack of needles and it looks like he's nearing his breaking point.

Behind the line, they are understaffed as well, and two guys are working like dogs, sweating like they have glandular disorders. Neither will look up at us, the ones desperately waiting for our food to come up. They know better.

One guy is working the grill, the oven, and the stovetop, darting back and forth, flipping steaks, tossing meat in sauce pans, and plopping raw chicken breasts onto the flat top. It looks like he has forty pieces of meat working, all in different stages of cooking, all of them requiring attention at separate moments. I have no idea how he keeps track of it all. If it were me back there, nothing would come out right.

The other guy is working the deep fryer, dropping and lifting baskets of fries, wings, and other deep-fried delicacies every forty seconds are so. He's also running the cold line, preparing salads, desserts, and some of the entrees and appetizers which don't require cooking. He's keeping up, but just barely.

The Mexican dishwasher brings stacks of freshly washed dishes at regular intervals and, every time he drops off a stack, they are gone in moments.

"I need fries to sell!"

"Turkey club on rye with wheels!"

"Four chicken and two burgers, all day!"

The stress in this room is palpable. You can feel it. You can reach out and touch it.

I called this place a zoo, but it isn't, not at all. It's an engine, and it's being pushed to its limits. The needle is buried in the red and this thing feels like it could blow a gasket at any second, but it doesn't.

It would only take one person, one meltdown, to send this place spiraling down until it crashed and burned into an explosion of fire and debris. Instead, every person mans up. They continue plugging away, one step at a time, flipping meat, scooping potatoes, prepping plates, and sending them out, barely finishing one ticket before three more come chugging off the printer.

I'm as stressed as anybody. My table has been waiting thirty minutes for a burger, a chicken sandwich, and a salad. They don't understand what's taking so long.

"How long does it take to cook a burger?"

Not long, but it does take a while to cook food for the 83 people who ordered five minutes before you.

I want to speak up, but I can't bring myself to do it. These guys have enough on their plate. It wouldn't do any good, anyway.

Instead, I go about preparing the condiments I'm going to need, ramekins of ketchup, mayonnaise, and ranch dressing. By the time my food is ready, I'm all set to go.

It would be an easy trek across the hotel if it was just my food, but two of the She Devils' orders are up, too. The manager loads my tray with more plates than are humanly possible to carry. Some of them are hanging half off the sides.

I slide the overloaded tray until just the far edge of it is resting on the stainless steel table. Hunching beside it and steadying it with my right hand, I reach under with my left, planting my palm firmly in the center. I take a deep breath and stand erect, balancing the awkward and heavy tray on my hand.

The front of the tray is heavier than the back, so I have to adjust my placement, working my hand slightly forward, until I can feel the balance fall into place.

"You got it?" my manager asks.

"Yeah," I reply. "I got it."

I start back toward the bar, paying close attention to the slight sway of the tray with every step I take, adjusting my hand placement to control the balance. All I can think of is Angie.

I think her name was Angie.

It was way back when I first started working at O'Brady's. Angie was a pretty young thing. She was a petite slice of feminine virtue with milk chocolate skin and piercing brown eyes. She had just made detective in the Baltimore City Police force so she was this sexy mix of street smart toughness and soft girlish features. Angie and her coworkers would stop by for drinks after their shift from time to time.

I was quite smitten with Angie.

One night, they were all sitting around a table talking about work, much like my friends and I like to do. There were seven of them and one of them ordered a round of drinks.

Being the young stud and super cool bartender I was in those days, I made the drinks in record time and placed them all on a small cocktail tray. I hoisted it up over my head and came strolling back to their table. I went straight to Angie.

"Ladies first," I probably said, lowering the tray and hovering it over her. Like I said, I was pretty smooth back then.

I reached down and took hold of her rum and coke, lifting it off and presenting it to her like it was a glass of fine wine. Unfortunately, when I removed her drink, it threw off the balance of the tray. I felt it wobble slightly and I panicked, over-compensating for the missing weight.

I can only imagine the look of horror on my face as the tray full of drinks went tumbling into the lap of my lovely Angie. It was a moment I will never forget and it's a moment I think about every time I lift a tray, even all these years later.

The long walk back to the bar is miserable. The muscles in my arm are screaming for relief, but I'm forced to hold it in place, terrified the slightest adjustment will send the whole thing toppling over. As I pass the front desk, I contemplate stopping, setting it down for a moment of rest, but I push on.

I'm the the Little Engine That Could as I trudge along.

I think I can.

I think I can.

I think I can.

There are two bowls of soup in the center of the tray and I can hear them sloshing about with every step. I can only hope there will still be some left in the bowls by the time they get to the table.

The bar is crazier than ever by the time I get there. There are more people standing around waiting for tables than there are eating. There is no end in sight to this madness.

People are glaring at me when I walk in, and I am desperate to set this heavy son of a bitch anywhere I can set it. They're looking at me like I'm covered in chocolate sauce. They're looking at me with the look of hungry, wild animals and they've detected the scent of blood on me.

The tray stand is on the far side of the bar and my arm feels like it could give out at any second. I'm loaded down like a pack mule, trying to weave my way through the crowd. Most of them just stand in my way, staring at me with blank looks on their faces. They're hunger zombies, incapable of doing anything as complicated as stepping out of my way.

Four feet away from the tray stand I hit a snag. It's a husband and wife and they're standing between me and my destination, that sacred spot where I can set down my load and relieve the pain in my arm and back.

From the looks of it, they've never been in a bar or restaurant before. Who am I kidding? They look like they were just dropped onto an alien planet. They're newborn fawns exploring the forest on their own for the first time.

Wide-eyed and scared, their heads turn this way and that,

trying to understand the confusion surrounding them. When they spot me, their eyes light up. I'm the port in the storm they've been looking for.

They're both talking at once, asking me every question they can think of.

"Do you work here?"

No, I bring my own tray of food to every restaurant I go to.

"Are you open?"

No sir. All these people are figments of your imagination.

"Can we get a table for two?"

Sure thing. We're a Viking-themed restaurant. Just pick a table you like and fight the current people to the death.

"I'll be with you in just a second," I grunt through the pain, sidestepping around them and trying to work my way to the stand. The couple is still asking me questions.

Two steps away, an unsupervised child darts across my path and I am forced to stop, dead in my tracks. My first instinct was to run him over, but I don't want to have to fill out the incident report.

As soon as I stop, I feel it. When I made the sudden stop, the momentum of the tray kept going, shifting all the plates forward. It was very slight and it happened in a split second, but I can feel the aftermath.

My balance is off. A flash of sheer terror washes through my brain.

Instinctively, I tip it back the other way, trying to compensate, searching for some kind of counter balance and regain control.

It starts with a wobble. It's hardly anything and I'm positive I can hold it together.

I am wrong.

As the tray of plates goes falling forward, I reach out, with my free hand, in a desperate attempt to catch it, but it's a useless gesture. It's akin to trying to fill a hot-air balloon with a bicycle pump.

I stand, paralyzed, watching helplessly as it goes crashing to the floor. It's an out-of-body experience and I watch it unfold in slow motion, panic and horror filling my mind.

When it hits the floor, it sounds like a bomb went off. Everyone stops what they're doing and looks up to see what the commotion is. Babies begin to cry. Mothers pull their small children in close, holding them tight for protection. Men with weak hearts grasp at their chests.

One jackass starts clapping.

It's Angie all over again, and my night is screwed.

What can I say? It's not all hot biker chicks on picnic tables. When the bottom falls out at my job, it falls out hard.

Sure, that is one of the more extreme examples, but there are plenty of factors that can screw up a perfectly good night. These factors can range from almost anything. The asshole customer is certainly the most common way to see your night go down the toilet, but he is, by no means, the only cause out there.

Maybe it's outside forces in your life bringing you down and wrecking your mood. Maybe it's an incompetent coworker, forcing you to work twice as hard as you need to. It could be the forces of nature working against you, or maybe the kitchen is having a bad night. Sometimes, it's just you. Sometimes, you're just out of sync and can't find your groove.

Let's take a look at a few. We'll start with that a-hole customer. They're always fun to talk about.

So, I'm working at the Big Digs one night. This one just happened recently, so it's still fresh in my mind. It's a fairly busy night and my bar is pretty full.

This guy comes in and takes a seat at the bar. He's a middle-aged ginger in a suit and tie and I can tell right away he's had a few drinks, but I decide he's not too drunk. He orders a beer and a seared tuna appetizer.

"How long will that take?" he asks.

Judging from the crowd and the average ticket times for the night, I tell him between ten and fifteen minutes.

Five minutes go by.

"Where's my appetizer?" he asks.

I assure him it is on the way.

Five more minutes.

"How long does it take to sear tuna?" he snaps. "You slap it down for thirty seconds and flip it over for another thirty."

I explain to him that his is not the only order back there and I assure him that his tuna will be out soon. This in no way appeases him. From here on out, he is calling me over, every thirty seconds, to bitch about how long his app is taking.

You have no idea how much fun this is.

This story is actually a combination of a couple of those factors that can come together to screw your night royally. Unbeknownst to me, the kitchen has run out of the Asian spices they use on the seared tuna and they are frantically trying to figure something out.

After fifteen minutes, this guy is about to lose his marbles. He keeps flagging me down to bitch me out over the insanely long time he's been waiting for his food.

I pick up a radio and call a manager. Yes, at the Big Digs hotel, we have high-speed walkie-talkies we use to communicate. I ask him to check up on my app and see what's taking so long.

Five more minutes go by.

By now, my guy is having a full-blown conniption fit. I'm trying my best to avoid him, but he keeps calling me over to ream me out because he's still waiting for his tuna.

"How long does it take to cook tuna?" he keeps yelling to me.

I keep apologizing for the wait and assuring him his appetizer is on the way. I get back on the radio. This time, my manager isn't answering. I'm on my own.

You have to remember, I still have a full bar of other people who want me to fetch various things for them. I'm trying my best to keep them happy while still swinging by Mister In-My-Face for another berating.

He is not a happy camper.

I try the radio two more times, but I get nothing. I call the front desk and tell them, "I need a manager to get back to me right away. I have a guy going ballistic over a piece of fish."

Finally, my manager calls me on the phone. He explains what's going on.

"Well, you need to either get his appetizer over here or come talk to him yourself. I'm getting tired of being bitched out."

I go back over to the guy. I even buy him a beer. I explain the situation and assure him my manager is working on it.

This information elevates him to an even higher level of pissed off. He is screaming at me that he's been waiting 45 minutes for an appetizer that should take five minutes. It's been twenty.

I apologize again and assure him that his appetizer will be out soon.

By this time, I'm doing my best to avoid him, concentrating on my other customers, but he is calling me back every twelve seconds for an update on his food and to rip me another new one. I'm getting a little frustrated.

I explain, again, that my manager is working on it. I also explain that I have done everything I can do, on my end, to get his food out as quickly as possible. My bar is busy and I'm all alone, so I can't leave to check on it. I have made four calls to find out what the hold up is and I've updated him on the status of the missing Asian spices. I apologize again and ask him what else he would like me to do. I also assure him that we will be taking care of his tab due to the inconvenience.

"How long does it take to cook tuna?" he keeps yelling. "I've been waiting an hour."

It's been 23 minutes, which, I agree, is a long time to wait for a piece of fish, but is nowhere close to an hour.

At this point, I take the radio into the back room and call my manager again.

"It's almost ready," he tells me.

"Bring it out raw if you have to," I reply. "I don't care. If this guy doesn't stop screaming in my face, I'm going to end up getting fired tonight, because I'm not going to take it much longer."

Two minutes later, my manager comes rushing into the bar with the missing tuna. He gives it to the guy and apologizes for the wait, explaining again the situation with the Asian spices.

The guy doesn't care. He wants to bitch more. It's my manager's turn to get reamed out.

Once my manager leaves, douche bag wolfs down his appetizer like he hasn't eaten in a week. When he's done, he calls me over again.

I'm thinking, he's fed, he's happy, he's getting a free tab. Everything is good, right?

Not even.

He wants to bitch more. He is recounting the whole ugly ordeal, only now it's an hour and a half he waited for his app. It was 26 minutes. We checked on the computer.

The guy is going off worse than ever. He is ranting and raving over the fish appetizer he's already finished and doesn't have to pay for. At some point, he starts calling me a liar.

I've had enough.

"How am I a liar?" I ask, in the most polite tone I can muster.

"You lied! You said it would take ten minutes."

It took everything I had not to lose my cool. I took a deep breath and said, "I told you ten to fifteen. When I put your order in, that was the best estimation I had. It took 26 minutes.

"I've apologized, over and over. When it took longer than

anticipated, I called over to the kitchen five times to find out what was going on. I bought you a beer and ended up taking care of your entire tab. What else would you like me to do?"

"How long does it take to cook tuna?" he yelled back.

"Sir, I'm not the one who cooked your app. I did everything I could do, on my end, to get you your tuna in as timely a manner as possible. I don't know what else you want from me."

Apparently, what he wanted from me was a turkey club sandwich, which he ordered next.

"I'd like it before the next two hours," he added.

Why a person would order more food from a restaurant he was so unhappy with, I have no idea.

After I rang in his order, I got back on the radio.

"If that turkey club takes more than ten minutes, I'm quitting," I told my manager.

It was out in five.

By the way, if you are a middle-aged ginger who was recently in a fancy hotel in Myrtle Beach and you ordered a seared tuna appetizer and it took 26 minutes and you bitched and yelled at the bartender like he was your dark-headed stepchild, I have one thing to say to you. You are a jackass of the highest caliber.

For the record, he jipped me on the tip, too. That was all right, though. I was just glad to be rid of him.

Needless to say, my night was ruined.

Look, I get that his tuna took a little longer than expected. I even get that he was upset. He had every right to be.

What I don't get is why a grown man would fly off the handle over a piece of fish. Is it really necessary to throw down over supper? What does a person like that do when something major goes wrong in his life? How does he react when his teenage son fails ninth-grade algebra? Excommunication from the family? Tar and feathers? Waterboarding?

Plus, like I mentioned earlier. You are bitching at the wrong person.

Am I saying I'm perfect, that I never make a mistake? Of course not. I'm only human. I make mistakes all the time. When I do, I don't think it's reason for a public lashing.

Speaking of mistakes, here's one we've all made in this business.

Forgetting an order.

What can I say? Contrary to popular belief, we are not machines.

At many restaurants and bars around the country, bartenders and servers are encouraged to write things down. In some places it is even required. In many, it is not.

At the Big Digs Hotel and at the Freedom Steakhouse and Brewery, no one ever wrote anything down. Sure, maybe if it was a particularly large table, but for the most part, we all take orders in our heads.

I can't tell you how many times I've approached a coworker at the computer and started to speak to them, only to get their palm in my face. This is not a rude gesture on their part. It simply means they have just taken a dinner order for their eight-top and are in the process of ringing it in, and if I say one single word, it is liable to turn all the organized tidbits of information in their head to mush.

My personal formula for remembering is pretty simple. I repeat the key points back to myself. This usually does the trick and I seldom forget anything.

For example, a dinner order might be a house salad with Italian dressing and a New York strip, medium-rare, with mashed potatoes. In my head, I would say, "Italian, mid-rare strip, mashed."

Simple stuff.

It is until it isn't.

This is another one of those moments that will screw up your night.

You've just taken an order for a six-top. You get back to the computer and you are ringing it in. Everything is going fine. You're in the zone. You're like a courthouse stenographer, typing away.

Ranch dressing, medium filet, fingerling potatoes.

Balsamic, roasted chicken, no tomato, rice.

Caesar, fish special, fingerlings.

Blue cheese, rare strip, mashed.

Kid burger, no cheese, fries.

Your fingers and brain are working as one as you are like a video gamer going for the high score. That is, until you get to the last order.

It was the sweet old lady, asking all the questions. She couldn't decide between the sea bass or the grouper. She was all set on the sea bass, but then switched to the grouper. Then she switched back.

Then she remembered she had fish for lunch and started looking at the chicken carbonara, but she wasn't sure if she was in the mood for pasta. She thought the bone-in pork chop sounded good, but she was afraid it would be too much food.

She wasn't very hungry, so she started looking at salads. She asked if she could get the chicken Caesar with salmon instead of chicken. At one point, she was considering the lobster cobb, but maybe a small house was all she needed.

The whole time she is going through this, you are trying to remember what the rest of her family ordered.

When you left her table, you had it all straight. You knew every person's order. You knew it when you started ringing it in. You had it completely, until you got to hers.

Now, your brain is in meltdown mode. It's a good thing you've already rung in the rest of the order or that would be lost, too. If someone were to ask you your name, there would be a 50/50 chance you could come up with it.

You look back at the table, trying to remember. You go through every person, replaying their orders in your head. You can hear their voices. You can recall every detail about every person, except her. With her, all you can remember is she's allergic to peanuts.

Okay, maybe this isn't going to ruin your whole night, but it still sucks. Nobody wants to screw up at work. We are professionals and, most of us, like to think we are good at what we do. Nobody wants to slink back over to a table to figure out what we forgot.

"Did you want the Caesar with salmon or the lobster cobb?"

"I wanted a turkey club, dumb ass."

Sometimes you don't realize you made the mistake until it's too late. The meal comes out and that one person is looking down at their plate like it's covered in worms.

"This isn't what I ordered!"

In this case, we always, 100 percent of the time, blame the kitchen.

"No, you most certainly did not. My kitchen must have sent out the wrong thing. I'll get that taken care of, right away. What was it you ordered?"

Of course, you don't tell the kitchen you threw them under the bus. With them, you tell them the guest changed her mind or she didn't like the looks of it.

They will be angry, of course, but you just shrug your shoulders and say, "What are you going to do? You know how people are."

You can't feel too guilty about doing this. After all, the kitchen will make plenty of mistakes and you will get your share of butt-chewings over their screw-ups. Think of it as a karma thing.

Besides, the kitchen doesn't work for tips, so who cares if the customer hates the kitchen staff? The main thing is to keep the customers on your side and let them see you are working to get things done the way they want.

"I'm so sorry about that. Some of those guys in the kitchen don't read so well."

Unfortunately, you can't always blame the kitchen. Sometimes you're just out of sync and can't find your rhythm. Sometimes, you are just out of it.

One time, at the Freedom Steakhouse and Brewery, I had a lady order a White Russian with Coke. I made her a White Russian and put Coke in it.

"No, this has milk in it," she told me. "I just want Coke."

I was having a bad day. I went back and made her the same thing.

"No, this has milk in it. I want it with Coke."

Now, I'm a reasonably intelligent guy. Substituting Coke for milk should not have been the brain-teaser that it turned out to be. That day, I just didn't have it. I made the exact same drink a third time.

I could point out what she wanted was a Black Russian with Coke. Milk is actually what makes a White Russian white, but the truth is, I should have been smart enough to figure out this mind-baffling mystery. That day, for whatever reason, I was not.

We've all done it.

This would be a good time to reiterate about those people who don't order things correctly. Now that I've shown myself in a bad light, let's go back and make fun of other people some more. Sure, I'm not perfect, but neither are the people I usually end up waiting on.

Here are some more things to avoid doing if you don't want to end up in a book like this.

I don't know why, but this one drives me crazy. It's people who order their drinks backward.

"I'd like a tonic and vodka and a Coke and rum."

Who does that?

Would you like a jelly and peanut butter sandwich to go with that?

It's like waiting on Yoda.

"Like I would, a tonic and vodka."

I had one guy order a Coke and Royal Crown. That's like the trifecta of getting it wrong. He was looking for a Crown Royal and Coke.

Here's one. You do not want a cheeseburger without cheese. That would be called a hamburger. The same thing goes for a hamburger with cheese. This is called a cheeseburger.

Also, if the menu states the burger comes with lettuce, tomato, onion and mayonnaise, you do not want a burger with lettuce, tomato and mayonnaise *only*. You can just say, "No onion."

"Can I get my drink in a plastic glass?"

Plastic? Glass? What is the magical substance of which you speak?

What you want is a plastic cup.

Remember, I have other people to get to and other things to fetch.

At the Big Digs, we do not have a hostess. People can come in and seat themselves. When I see people wandering around the bar with confused looks, I tell them they can have a seat wherever they like.

Usually, they respond with, "Anywhere?"

Well, yeah, unless someone else is already sitting there.

Sometimes they ask, "How about outside?"

Yeah, I think that "anywhere" covers the outside, too.

Sometimes, people don't think about the questions they ask.

"Can I get a large Pepsi?"

Ma'am, this is a Four Diamond resort. We don't supersize meals.

Slightly off topic, if we are having a conversation, please try to concentrate. If you go to ask me a question, and your mind wanders halfway through, I have no idea how to answer you.

"Does the salmon purse..."

Yes, it does. Twice on Sundays.

Maybe you are just a long thinker. I love these people, especially when I'm in the weeds.

If you are one of these people, that's fine. Take all the time you need. Just don't call me over to watch you mull over your decision like you are buying a house. Again, I have things I could be doing.

Okay, you're out for a night on the town and you're looking to live it up. Maybe you're looking to try something new. Please, please, please, do not make me stand there while you scroll through your phone looking for some drink I've never heard of.

Once you find it, I will be happy to make it for you, but I do not want to watch you scour the internet for a drink called a Purple Neon Plum Picker.

While we are on the topic of phones, I get it. It's the world we live in. If that phone call you are on is so important, by all means, go right ahead. Just don't call me over to listen to you catch up with your Aunt Bessie. I will be happy to come back when you are finished.

Don't even get me started on Bluetooth headsets. I have no idea how many people I've answered who were actually talking to someone three states away. I guess that one has more to do with the world we live in.

As I stated earlier, it's not just the customers experiencing brain farts. We do it all the time.

This is one my favorite She Devil told me. Her name is Lauren, and no, she's not the Freedom Steakhouse girl who brought back the can of steam.

Lauren was working the Big Digs on a busy night. Her section was full and she was running around, trying to keep on top of things. She was walking toward two of her tables. One of them had just been seated and the other had just gotten their food.

In her mind, she was preparing herself to greet each table.

The first one she was going to start off with, "I'm Lauren."

The other one she was going to ask if everything was good.

Instead, she approached her table and said, "I'm God."

Wow. Nice to meet you, God. I've heard so much about you.

This one just happened and I found it pretty funny. It's another server not using her noggin.

We had a new girl working at the Big Digs. She had just finished training and was working one of her first shifts on the floor alone. Someone at her table ordered an Irish Coffee with no sugar and no cream.

Now, at the Big Digs, our standard Irish Coffee consists of Irish whiskey, brown sugar, and whipped cream, so I poured a shot of Jameson into a clear coffee mug and sat it at the service bar. At our place, the She Devils add their own coffee to their drinks so it doesn't get cold before they drop it off.

I heard the girl ask me something about her drink, but I was busy with another customer. Over my shoulder, I told her, "Just put coffee in it."

She took it to her table, as it was.

A minute later, she was back at the service bar with a confused look on her face, holding her clear glass with a shot of whiskey in it.

"I thought you told me you added the coffee," she said.

All I could do was look at her. "Do you know what coffee looks like?"

Oh, well. We've all been there. At least she didn't take it over there three times.

I digress. We were talking about things that screw up your night, not things that annoy you. If I were still talking about annoying people, I might mention the modifiers and deconstructors, the people who have to take every item on the menu and reinvent it to fit their own twisted desires.

"I'll take the tuna salad sandwich, but hold the tuna and add egg, salmon, and bacon. I'd also like to get it with bacon, basil, and sliced cucumbers."

I'm pretty sure that's not a tuna salad sandwich anymore.

Or I might even mention the soft talkers and mumblers who make my life a living hell.

Speak up like you've got a pair!

Or the people who find it necessary to change tables three times.

What is this, Goldie Locks and the Three Bears?

Or the people who tell me they absolutely must have four olives in their martini and when I take away their empty glass there are still four olives in it.

Do you just like the way they look?

What about the people who raise their hands to ask you a question like I'm their third-grade schoolteacher?

If you're going to ask if you can go potty, I should warn you, I'm probably going to say no.

That's just weird.

How about the large group that comes to your bar and insists on hanging out in the doorway where no one can get by them even though the entire restaurant is empty?

Or the Sports Dorks. Those are some of my favorites.

I get it. Your game comes on in an hour and a half. You do not need to keep asking me every ten minutes if I'm going to put the game on.

Look, I like my team too. That doesn't mean if I'm sitting at a bar by myself I'm going to jump up and down, hooting and hollering every time my team gets a first down. You are a grown man and that's just annoying.

I will let you in on a little secret, too. I am secretly hoping your team gets the tar beat out of it. Every time the other team scores, or your team fumbles the ball, I am smiling inside. I can't help it.

Speaking of Sports Dorks, if you come to my bar and fifteen people are watching the Ohio State and Michigan game, there is a good chance I am not going to change it to East Lafayette Technical College vs. Southwest Rhode Island State just because you went to school there.

If you can find a TV that is not being watched, I will be happy to put your game on, but the truth is, nobody else cares. In fact, even if I concentrated all my energy and summoned all the willpower I had, I couldn't make myself care any less.

Oops. I got off track again, didn't I?

We were talking about bad days in the bar and restaurant business. It's coming back to me.

This is a story that always stuck with me.

I used to know this girl. She was a pretty blonde with a perky personality and a friendly demeanor. She was working at a busy Italian restaurant and the place was packed. Like many restaurants, they gave away free loaves of bread while you were waiting for your meal.

She was waiting on a large family and had already taken their dinner orders and served up some loaves of bread. The family wolfed it down like rats on a chicken carcass. The father then called her over and requested more bread.

"Sure," she said. "No problem." She went on to explain how it was a very busy night and they were momentarily out, but that more was cooking and she would bring some out as soon as it was ready.

"We need bread, now," the man replied.

Again, she assured him, as soon as it was up, she would be sure to bring him more bread.

The guy started bitching.

The girl apologized for the inconvenience and promised to bring them bread as soon as possible.

The guy bitched more.

As soon as she was gone, the guy continued ranting on about it. He was going on about what a crappy restaurant they were in and what a lousy server they were stuck with. At one point, he was making jokes, calling her stupid and incompetent, because she couldn't manage a task as simple as dropping off some bread.

What this guy didn't know was the girl's father and family were sitting at the next table and overheard the entire exchange. I can only imagine her father sat and took it as long as he could, listening to some knucklehead belittle his little girl.

Finally, he turned to the guy and said, "Look, what do you want her to do? She said she'd bring the bread out when it was ready."

Jerk off took offense. "I don't see where it's any of your concern."

"Well, I don't see where you get off calling that poor girl stupid."

The next thing you know, the two men were in each others' faces, about to go blow-to-blow. A manager had to come break it up.

The girl was in the back in tears, humiliated by the ordeal.

And all that over some free bread. I just don't get it.

Her night was ruined.

Here's another night that got ruined, but for a different reason.

I have another good friend who worked at a restaurant in North Myrtle Beach. It's a big chain across the country, and there might be one near you. For legal reasons, we will call it Rick's First Resort.

Rick's has this shtick. When you go in there, you are insulted and made fun of by your bartenders and servers. They even force you to wear paper dunce caps during your meal. It's all in fun and people love it, coming from all over to be insulted by the staff of Rick's First Resort.

My friend, we will call her Gretta, had been working there for a while. The thing you have to know about Gretta is she's actually very sweet and never had a bad word to say about anyone.

The management used to get on her about this.

"Come on, Gretta. You have to get into the spirit of it. Have some fun with it and get some zingers in."

One night, Gretta gets a table of golfers. There are like nine of them and she decides she's going to try her best to throw out some putdowns. There's one guy at the table who has kind of a messed-up hair cut. It's all short and choppy and looks uneven in spots. Gretta decides she's found her target.

"Did you get a free bowl of soup with that haircut?"

"Do that yourself, did ya?"

"What happened? Did your flowbie break down halfway into it?"

Nobody at the table is laughing. Gretta can't understand. She thought she did exactly what they wanted.

She went back to the computer and began ringing in their orders. A minute later, one of the guys from her table approaches.

"Hey, look," he says, "Our buddy has had a rough time lately. He recently finished with a round of chemotherapy and he's kind of sensitive about his hair. Could you take it easy on him?"

She was beyond mortified. I don't think she ever tried to insult another person again.

Her night was ruined.

To her credit, she went back to the table and apologized. By the end of the night, they loved her.

It seems like this chapter has a darker feel to it than some of the others, but dark doesn't scare me. I embrace the dark.

This might be a good time to tell you how I got the job at Hull Street Blues. It's a bit more than a bad day story, but it kind of fits with the theme we have going. It also says a little about the lifestyle that comes with this job.

I had put in my notice at O'Brady's and had been hanging out at Hull Street with some friends. One of them mentioned how I should get a job there. This sounded good to me, as Hull Street seemed like a much hipper bar with a younger crowd, and they had a lot more going on, such as live music.

After putting in my notice, I went into Hull Street and was sitting at the bar, having a beer and trying to think of how to approach the subject. Danny, the owner, came up to me and said, "So, I hear you're going to come and join us."

My friend had already mentioned it to him. It was one of the easiest job interviews I ever had.

The only problem was Hull Street had a full staff and they really didn't have any shifts available. Danny promised to try and work me into the schedule.

The next night, I came back into the bar and hung out 'til closing time. I had a mutual friend with one of the bartenders working that night.

To protect his reputation and keep from embarrassing him, we will call him Harry.

Harry worked there part time and was closing with a guy named Hugh who worked there five nights a week.

After they closed up, the three of us got some beer and went back to my apartment for some late-night partying. We were back at my place when Hugh produced the largest bag of cocaine that I have ever seen in my life. It wasn't like a little sandwich bag. It was one of those jumbo freezer bags and it was half full.

I can only guess it must have been like $15,000 worth of coke, but I am mostly basing this on various episodes of "Miami Vice," as I have no idea. It was like that scene from "Scarface" where Pacino sticks his face in the pile of cocaine.

Don't judge me. It was the '80s and everybody was doing it.

This would probably be a good time to say that I, in no way, promote the use of illegal drugs. Over the years, I have experimented with plenty of drugs, but I've never really considered myself a druggie. I was always much more of a casual user and I never did much more than dabble here and there.

Especially where cocaine is concerned. Out of all the drugs I've ever tried, cocaine was one of my least favorites. For me it just made me want to stay up all night and talk a lot. The thing is, I can do all that on beer and it's a lot cheaper.

So, Harry, Hugh, and I are sitting around in my apartment drinking beer, listening to Elvis Costello and talking about everything under the sun when I happen to glance up at the clock. It's 12:30.

12:30 p.m.

They closed the bar at 2 a.m.

We had been sitting around drinking and snorting cocaine for ten and a half hours.

I looked back at my new best friends and I think I said something like, "This has been fun and all, but you two need to get the hell out of my apartment."

They looked at me like I was crazy.

"I'm not kidding. You guys need to leave."

"Why?"

"Why? Because it's 12:30. Because the sun is shining and none of us have been to sleep in over 24 hours. Because, if I do one more line of coke, my head is going to cave in and my heart is going to explode inside my chest."

This seemed like good reasoning to Harry and Hugh and they made their hasty exit. I'm guessing it was another three hours before I could finally pass out.

The other thing about cocaine is it really screws with you in almost every way possible. I have one friend who liked to say, "I hate cocaine, but I love the way it smells."

If you have never done cocaine, consider yourself lucky. It sucks.

For me, I feel like garbage for two days after. I'm tired, listless, and out of whack, and I am overcome by this deep-rooted, chemical-induced depression. This is usually combined with the fact I'm kicking myself in the ass for staying up too late and spending too much money. Sounds fun, huh?

Somehow, I manage to drag my ass out of bed around eight o'clock that night. I find some books Hugh left in my living room and I'm feeling a little guilty for the way I kicked out my two new buddies. I knew Hugh would be working that night so I gather his things and head down to Hull Street.

Hugh is not there. Instead, Danny's girlfriend (who worked days) is behind the bar, pulling a double.

"When did you see Hugh?" she asks.

"Last night."

"Was Harry with him?"

"Yeah."

She gets on the phone and calls Danny, who rushes over.

"When did you see Hugh?" he asks me when he gets there.

"Last night."

"Was Harry with him?"

"Yeah."

It turns out, after they closed the bar, Hugh decided to help himself to all the money in the cash register and pull a disappearing act. Harry turned up two days later, after a 48-hour binge. They had ended up on some Russian freight ship partying with Soviet sailors. No lie.

Nobody ever heard from Hugh again, to my knowledge. He bolted town.

I took over the shift from Danny's girlfriend that night so she wouldn't have to pull a double, and from that moment on, I was a full-time employee at Hull Street Blues. Harry and I both felt terrible that we had been out partying with the guy who ripped off the bar, but neither of us had a clue. To Danny's credit, he never held it against us.

For months after, guys in suits came in looking for Hugh. They did not look happy. They would leave a number and tell us to call if we heard from him. I can only guess that Danny wasn't the only person he ripped off before skipping town. I'm sure the monster bag of cocaine had something to do with it, and if those people were ever able to track Hugh down, it wasn't going to be pretty. He could be at the bottom of the ocean in cement shoes, for all I know.

I worked with Harry for years after and he was one of my favorite people of all time. When things would get busy he loved to tell people, "I only have two hands and I can only do five things at once."

He was losing his hair and he would always say, "I have wavy hair. It's waving goodbye."

He'd always joke about how lonely he was and how he woke up like an airplane pilot every morning. The joke being his penis was like the airplane steering rod and he would mime steering, with his other arm out like an airplane wing.

He said he drove a pick-up truck because it was the only thing big enough to transport the large women he occasionally went home with and he would finish it off with a, "Big girls need love, too."

Whenever he saw a woman with large breasts, he loved to tell us how it was his dream to, one day, run barefoot through a whole field of *those*.

Harry was a lot of fun and I miss him. I hope hes doing well these days.

He was an electrician by trade and he worked part time at Hull Street for fun and a little extra cash, but he really liked the lifestyle that came along with it. He really liked cocaine, too. Much more than I ever did. I would try to hang with him, but I rarely could.

He was an usher at my wedding and I don't think he had been to sleep for 48 hours. It was very common for Harry to stay up and party for two days at a time. He was older than me, roughly about the age I am now, but he could party with the best of them. Back then, I think we all thought that was a good thing. We were stupid.

Harry got to where he was partying all the time. Five or six days a week. He was also the kind of guy who insisted on paying for everything when we were all out. If he didn't have cash, he would put it on a credit card. It got to where he started buying coke with money he charged to his card. Before long, he was in debt beyond his means and he came close to losing his home over drugs.

His younger brother had to bail him out so his house wasn't

foreclosed on. It must have been humiliating to go to his younger brother for help. Harry was a very proud guy.

The last I heard, Harry had given up drugs and booze and settled down with a nice girl he had dated in high school. He was out of the bar business, back to electrical work, and he was busy putting his life back together. God bless him. I really do miss him.

This next story is only medium dark, nothing compared to the last one.

There is this place I hang out at in Myrtle Beach. It's a great little bar with a neighborhood feel and everybody knows pretty much everyone who walks through the door. Again, I'm not sure this will be the most flattering story so maybe I will go with a fake name for it. How about if we call it the Australian Beer Bar?

Now, the Australian Beer Bar is a great place where everybody has a good time. The problem with working in a place like that is it's easy to forget you're at work. Sometimes you can find yourself getting sucked into the party. It's a little like me at Hull Street.

Now that I think of it, I have two quick stories about the Australian Beer Bar that kind of fit with this chapter.

The Australian Beer Bar is owned by a couple from up north. They have always been very fortunate with their help and some of the best bartenders I've known have worked there over the years.

But like I said, it's easy to get sucked into the lifestyle.

There was one guy who tended bar there. He didn't mind having a few cocktails throughout his shift. Near the end of his tenure at the Australian Beer Bar, he was getting a little out of hand.

One morning, one of the owners came in to open up and she found the back door wide open. The money was still in the cash register and the place hadn't been cleaned up from the night before. There was no sign of the bartender.

The owner didn't know what to think. She feared the worst and she called her husband, who rushed over. The two searched the bar and grounds for any sign of what had happened.

Out the back door and off to the side was a mound of sand. On the far side of it, the owners found their bartender. He was passed out, face down, with a garbage bag in his hand. While taking out the trash, he stumbled in the sand and passed out drunk.

Needless to say, it was his last shift at the Australian Beer Bar.

In an odd coincidence, there was another bartender at the Australian Beer Bar who I was actually very good friends with. I still am. On another morning, the owner came in to open up and she, again, found the door wide open. Like before, the money was still in the cash register, the place hadn't been cleaned, and there was no sign of the bartender. This time, however, the bartender's best friend was passed out cold on top of the pool table. The bartender had gone home after having too much to drink.

Needless to say, it was my friend's last shift at the Australian Beer Bar.

It's too bad. Both were very nice guys and good bartenders.

I am happy to report that both guys are doing fine these days and have straightened out their acts. The first guy got out of the bar business altogether and the second guy is tending bar at another establishment, but he no longer drinks behind the bar.

This next story I heard secondhand, but it's pretty classic nonetheless.

There was this guy and he was working at this restaurant and he had the day off. So, this guy proceeds to spend his entire day off doing what it is that restaurant people love to do; getting plastered. He ends up back at the restaurant he works at later that evening for drinks at the bar.

The GM of the restaurant is busy and not paying him much attention when a customer comes up to complain there is a naked man in the ladies' room. It just so happens there was a group of transvestites at the bar that night and he figures it must be a misunderstanding involving one of them so he goes to check it out.

Entering the ladies' room, he finds one of the stalls locked and he gets no answer from whoever is inside. He gets down and peers under the door to find his off-duty employee curled up and sleeping buck naked beside the commode. The guy's clothes are all neatly folded and piled on the back of the toilet seat.

They get the guy awake and dressed and they put him in a cab and send him home, but apparently the guy decided he hadn't had quite enough. The next morning, the GM gets a call from the guy.

"Was I in there last night?" the guy asks. "I seem to vaguely remember being there and I just woke up, down by the beach in the backseat of a car I have never seen before."

"You were here, all right," the GM says, explaining to the bewildered guy what had taken place.

"Do I still have a job?" the guy asks.

"No. I'm afraid not."

That's how you go and get yourself fired on your day off, not an easy thing to accomplish.

Somehow, in this chapter, we've managed to go from bad days

and nights to bad choices, from your night turning sour to the lifestyle catching up to you. This seems perfectly natural to me.

It's a lot like the business itself. Everything can be rolling along fine, when *wham*. Somebody throws you a curve ball. Your night is screwed. You're out of a job. You have an expensive cocaine habit. You just never know.

I began this chapter with a story of me breaking a tray full of plates. I'll leave it with me breaking a rack full of glasses.

It was my early days at the Freedom Steakhouse and Brewery. I was working a lunch shift with one of my good friends and we were slammed. We were running low on glasses so I ran back to the dish room to grab a rack of clean ones.

As I came jogging back out to the bar, the handle on the rack was busted and gave way, sending the rack crashing to the floor. There were bits and pieces of glass everywhere and I went about cleaning it up. My friend came over and was trying to help.

About this time, our GM came walking over. "That money is already gone," he said.

He pointed to the crowded barroom. "Let's worry about that money now."

He was right. Sometimes, you just have to pick yourself up by the bootstraps and carry on.

CHAPTER EIGHT
PUT A CORK IN IT

The hours can be grueling. The money is hit or miss. The busy times can be almost more than humanly possible to handle and the slow times can be like Chinese water torture. Then, of course ... there are the people.

Here's one. I'm throwing this in because it happened just yesterday and it's still fresh in my mind.

I was working a day shift with one of the She Devils. It was one of those beautiful spring days we sometimes get in the middle of March in Myrtle Beach. In other words, we were understaffed and slammed.

Both of us were running around like chickens with our heads cut off. In the middle of the madness, a woman comes in alone. She sits in the She Devil's section out on the back balcony and proceeds to order the lobster cobb salad, hold the bacon and dressing.

First off, it is the bacon and dressing that give the lobster cobb salad its flavor. The dressing is also what holds it together and makes for the impressive presentation when it comes out in tower form.

Without the dressing, it is basically a plate of lettuce, tomato and lobster bits.

This woman is horrified. First off, it's bland and tasteless. Secondly, she says, it looks disgusting.

I don't know how disgusting a plate of fresh lettuce, tomatoes and lobster bits can look, but what do I know?

The She Devil apologizes, for what? I have no idea. She then offers to bring the woman a menu so she can pick out something else.

"No," the woman responds with a huff. "I don't want anything else. My confidence is shattered."

Okay, drama queen, bring it down a few notches.

Really? Your confidence is shattered?

Judging from the size of her, I'm fairly confident her confidence returned before the next meal-time rolled around.

Like I said ... the people.

Here's another one that happens all the time and I just don't get it. At the Big Digs we have two large-screen TVs on the side wall. They sit, maybe, a foot and half from each other, side by side, and there are tables scattered about beneath them.

Usually, we have two different games playing on them at any given time. I wish I had a nickel for every person who has sat down at one of the tables and requested we change the TV closest to them to the exact same game that is playing on the other television.

Now, you have to understand, *these TVs are side by side.* A person wouldn't even have to turn their head to see the other TV. They would just have to avert their eyes, slightly, to one side. Apparently, this is too much trouble.

Like I said, I don't get it.

Fortunately, for the sake of our sanity, the people make up just a part of what we do. Through out it all, we still manage to have a little fun along the way.

Maybe my least favorite restaurant tradition occurs when someone leaves. When they have put in their notice and are going on to a new job or heading back to school after working in the restaurant for the summer.

Basically, on this person's last day, all of their friends and coworkers get together and create a very special concoction. This concoction can consist of any of the following ingredients: cooking oil, whipped cream, peanut butter, bacon fat, flour, gravy, chocolate sauce, and/or maple syrup. Usually the final product will contain an assortment of many of the above, but I have seen some creative people add others to it as well.

These ingredients are mixed together and placed in an array of carriers. Foil pie pans and coffee filters seem to work the best.

At an allotted time at the end of the person's shift, everyone will gather their containers of slop together and sneak up behind the person before pelting and smearing them with this messy, smelly, and sticky substance. This practice is not considered a success unless the victim ends up with the stuff caked into their hair, ears and, eyes, and their clothes are covered in the slime.

One particularly good one occurred at the Freedom Steakhouse and Brewery. Our GM, Billy, was moving on to another job and some of our staff decided to get him good. They created an abnormally foul version of this concoction and placed it in a five-gallon bucket.

Then they took the bucket of slop up on the roof and left it out in the hot sun to simmer and ferment for two days.

The plan was to sneak up to the roof and ration it out before sneaking up on Billy and covering him in it.

Billy knew something was up, though, and was extremely paranoid for the last few days of his Freedom Steakhouse and Brewery career, and he scoured the restaurant in search of any clues to what might be going on behind his back. On the morning of his last shift he wandered up onto the roof (where no one ever goes).

He found the horrendous smelling bucket and he put two and two together.

What he did next was nothing short of genius.

Using some rope and wire, he rigged the bucket at the top of the roof door so that whoever opened it would have the bucket of goo come falling down and splattering over them. This is like MacGyver type stuff!

His plan was, when the group of conspirators came to fetch their swill, they would fall into his trap and would be ambushed by their own doing. This was a great plan but with one problem.

On the morning they were going to carry out their plan, one of the hooligans decided to call up the restaurant and ask Matt, our kitchen manager, to check on the bucket and make sure it was approaching the retched consistency they were shooting for.

Now, Matt, to this point, knew nothing of the plot against Billy, but when he heard about it he thought it was funny as hell. He couldn't wait to see for himself what kind of thick rancid glop they had cooked up.

You can imagine his surprise when he opened the door.

Matt had to go home, shower, and change. He had to wash his clothes three times to get the smell out.

I said earlier this was one of my least favorite traditions. That isn't exactly true. I'm fine with it as long as I'm not the one getting pelted with crap.

People who work in this business love a good practical joke. Because we work in the food industry, there is a very good chance that food will be involved somewhere.

Here are some good ones I've either seen or heard about.

In restaurants, we are all surrounded by wonderful edibles, and this is a constant source of stress for managers. The trick is to try and keep your employees from eating up all of your profits. Most restaurants give their employees discounts on food and some will provide a meal for every shift a person works, but this isn't always the case. Even if it were, employees would always be plotting ways to get free food.

In one restaurant (which will remain nameless) a general manager kept noticing his employees were sneaking pieces of cheesecake and setting them off to the side, nibbling on them as they went. This probably wasn't just one employee as, when this occurs, you usually have a few sharing an item and taking a bite here and there.

This GM went off to the kitchen and got a block of butter. He then cut it into a perfect triangle before caking the bottom with crushed cornflakes to make it look like crust. Next, he covered it with fresh strawberries and whipped cream and sat it back where his servers were stashing their snacks. From there he just had to sit back and wait until his mousetrap caught him a mouse.

Have you ever bit into a stick of butter? It wasn't difficult to spot the guilty party. It was the one running for the bathroom and gagging.

Another GM had the same idea. He took a slice of his restaurant's homemade apple pie and heated it up just right before adding his special *a la mode* to top it off. Instead of ice cream, he placed an ice-cold scoop of cooking lard on top of it. Boy, I bet that hit the spot. It gives a whole new meaning to I scream, you scream …

At still another restaurant, an employee turned the corner to find a steaming plate of fried coconut shrimp. They were golden crispy and piping hot and there were like ten of them there so he figured why not help himself to one? Who's going to know?

The problem was, it wasn't actually shrimp. The kitchen manager had cut off some prime rib fat and rolled it in coconut shrimp breading before deep-frying it. He even went to the trouble of sticking a shrimp tail out of it. Yummy.

Speaking of shrimp, one of those GMs also brought in a ball of Wasabi mustard from a sushi restaurant and molded it into a dozen bite-sized shrimps. He then rolled them in breading, deep fried them, and left them in the back of the restaurant with a side of cocktail sauce. This one could fall into the cruel and unusual punishment category.

I'm not sure I could even imagine biting into a wad of fried Wasabi. I tear up just thinking of it.

This stuff goes on constantly in restaurants all across America (maybe the world) and it is a constant source of amusement for people with juvenile sense of humors, such as myself.

You might be wondering how all those keen, experienced restaurant employees keep falling for the food pranks. It's simple. We all love to eat.

Well, everybody loves to eat!

No, seriously. You have no idea. We really, really, love to eat.

I will let you in on another little secret. We are not so crazy about paying for food.

You might think that being surrounded by the same food, day after day, would turn us off on our restaurant's particular dishes. To some degree. Of course. Even with my 50% employee discount, I'm dishing out my hard earned money unless I'm about to keel over from starvation.

Now, if that same food is free for the taking, that's a different story. Bring it on.

You might be wondering how a person goes about getting free food in the workplace. There are actually a number of ways.

I have seen people eat left over food directly off of customer's plates but this is a very rare and extremely disgusting occurrence. You usually only see this from dishwashers who are new to our country and are still in a state of shock over the amount of waste they witness in their new work environment. After a few thousand half eaten burgers come through their dish pit they put a halt to that nonsense and become as picky as the rest of us.

Another way to get free food is in the form of a bribe. Every restaurant manager holds this ace up his or her sleeve until they really need it, as they understand how much we love our free food.

"So and so called out sick tonight. I'm going to need you to stay and work a double."

"I can't. I have big plans with my family."

"I'll tell you what, I'll buy you dinner."

"OK!"

With our employee discount, this pretty much constitutes us selling away eight hours of our lives for $6, but what can I say? The mere thought of free food robs us of all common sense and makes rational decision making near impossible. Managers know this and they use it against us.

The most common and rewarding way to get free food in the restaurant you work is when food is sent back. This can be a mistake by the server, a foul up by the kitchen staff or some sort of mis-communication somewhere in the system. Whatever the circumstance, it's like the heavens opened up and laid a golden gift at our feet.

Every kitchen in America has that one spot on that one counter where the mistakes are placed through out the evening. This is the most revered and cherished spot in the building.

We walk by that spot all night long, eying it up, longingly waiting with watering mouths for something, anything, to be placed on that hollowed ground.

Finally, half way through the dinner rush, somebody screws up. A Fetticini Alfredo was supposed to be vegetarian but it went out with chicken. It's fresh off the stove and piping hot and I know it wont last long, even with most of the staff in the weeds. I rush over to the dish pit to drop off dirty plates.

"Bon Appetite, Miguel."

On the way back, I swing by and grab a clean fork, forgoing a plate, as I know I don't have time to sit down and enjoy so I'll just grab a quick bite. I'm back in twenty three seconds but, already, it's too late.

The once beautiful dish of pasta looks like a family of gorillas fought over it. Half eaten noodles lay draped over the edge of the plate. Alfredo sauce is splattered across the counter top and fourteen dirty forks are discarded about the surface. Surprisingly, the bottom of the bowl is spotless, like it was licked clean. It probably was.

Darn! Foiled again. I'll have to be quicker for round two,

The restaurant is quieter the next time it happens, as the dinner rush is winding down. Some of us are gathered by the food window, waiting on orders, when the assistant kitchen manager walks by with a plate of the meatloaf special. We all know where he's heading.

The room goes silent. Each of us are glancing at the other, trying to determine how to get the advantage in the mad dash for the free food. I consider shoving the new girl toward the hot grill but decide it might be a little drastic. I'm not sure it would buy me enough time, anyway.

We each begin to maneuver ourselves closer to the sacred counter top, slow and casual, as not to alert those unaware that free food is on the way. By the time he gets to the counter, the AKM is completely surrounded. People are reaching for it before he can set it down, foregoing forks and tearing at it with their bare hands. He's lucky to get away with all his fingers. The staff is on it like a school of piranhas on a baby lamb. It's not a pretty sight.

Okay, maybe I'm exaggerating a tad. I've been known to stretch the truth to make a point, from time to time. Then again, you might be surprised at just how accurate my descriptions are to what really goes on. We do love our free foodAll that food talk reminds me of another story. It's slightly off topic and it just barely fits in with our restaurant theme, but I love it, so here it goes.

I have these friends who run a fish market in town. One day, this couple comes in and buys a pound of shrimp. They get it, pay for it, and take it home.

The next day, the couple shows back up at the fish market. They are not happy with their purchase from the previous day.

"There's something wrong with the shrimp you sold us," they say. "It tasted awful and it was tough and chewy."

My friend was quite surprised and she asked them, "Well, how did you cook it?"

The couple's eyes got wide. "Cook it?"

I love that story. Can't you just picture the confused couple, sitting around their kitchen table, chomping away on their raw shrimp?

Priceless.

Okay, back to the restaurant stuff.

Another rule of thumb in the restaurant industry is to never leave your drink unattended. By this, I'm referring to the Diet Coke or sweet tea you just poured yourself. There is a very good chance that, when you get back to it, someone has added hot sauce, Worcestershire, or a half-cup of pepper to it. This can come as quite a shock if you aren't expecting it. This is also why you rarely see your bartender make himself or herself an entire glass of anything. He usually fills it part of the way before drinking it and discarding it into the dishwasher when he is done. There's no reason to take any chances.

Another thing you don't want to leave lying around are your car keys. Moving a person's car to the far side of the parking lot is another favorite practical joke in the service industry. It's a bitch getting off work, after a long night, and having to spend a half an hour looking for your car.

Of course, if it's your car they're after, they don't really need to have your keys to play their pranks. I have seen car door handles coated in whipped cream, chocolate sauce, honey, and all sorts of sticky substances which caused the driver considerable stress (especially after the restaurant has closed and there is nowhere to wash your hands).

I have also seen people's cars covered with just about everything you can imagine. Stupid bumper stickers added to unsuspecting car owners' vehicles are another favorite pastime.

The kitchen staff at the Freedom Steakhouse and Brewery used to love to put Dallas Cowboys bumper stickers on my Jeep and wait to see how long before I noticed. As a lifelong Redskins fan, you can imagine my horror when I realized I'd been driving around town, sporting the dreaded star on my bumper.

Dorks.

I will point out that these practical jokes are always geared toward people who work in the restaurant and I have never heard of anyone pulling one of these pranks on a customer. You can feel safe that this stuff will never happen to you when you go out to eat.

If it did, I would take it as the highest of compliments and it would mean the staff does not consider you a mere customer. If you end up on the business end of one of these babies, you can rest assured that you are considered family.

Speaking of family, I've barely mentioned the red-headed

stepchildren of our extended restaurant family. Of course, I'm referring to the kitchen staff. I should preface this by saying I have never worked in a kitchen before, but when I started working at Hull Street Blues, we were required to do our own food at the bar. This was an incredible pain in the ass and it was the quickest way to find yourself neck deep in the weeds.

Luckily, the menu wasn't very elaborate. It mostly included cold sandwiches, steamed shrimp and a few other easier things to prepare. On the bad side, it also included pizzas, which we prepared almost from scratch, rolling out the dough, and adding the sauce, cheese, and toppings. Three pizzas in a fifteen-minute span would place you in the deepest weeds imaginable.

Obviously, I am no expert on life in a restaurant kitchen and I will leave it to someone else to write the definitive book on life behind grills. I'm just going to take a second to comment on the people who work back there.

I will start out by saying that many people are under the impression that people who work in the kitchen are crackheads, dopers, and derelicts. This is mainly because a large portion of the people who work in the kitchen are crackheads, dopers, and derelicts.

This may not always be the case and I have known a great number of kitchen personnel who were not only wonderful people, but were straight as arrows. The thing is, if you *were* a crackhead, doper, or derelict, what better place to hide you away than the back of the house where none of the customers ever see you?

Now, don't get me wrong. The front of the house has more than its share of people who fit this description, too, but people like this who work with the public tend to be much better at hiding their various indiscretions.

The truth is, people who work in the kitchen actually tend to be very responsible, hardworking individuals. The ones who aren't are usually weeded out very quickly.

A good kitchen is the difference between someone like me making a good living or struggling to make ends meet. It is what makes or breaks your place. If your food sucks, nobody is coming to your restaurant, no matter how good your service is or how cheap your drink prices are.

I have known many great people who have worked their asses off in the kitchen, and I have always had a great respect for those who do it well. It certainly isn't an easy job.

The hours are long and the work can be monotonous and grueling. How would you like to stand over a 500-degree grill for eight hours a day? I would probably end up putting a pistol in my mouth.

They are the highest hourly paid employees in the restaurant for good reason, but while their money may be steadier than mine, they have little chance of having the big-money nights I am capable of earning. I guess that's the trade off; working in the kitchen certainly offers a stability that mine doesn't. Maybe it's why the gamblers of the world seem to be attracted to the front of the house.

Overall, I can't think of much bad to say about the kitchen guys except to say that, for some ungodly reason, the kitchen seems to attract an abnormal amount of Dallas Cowboys fans, as I mentioned earlier. As a lifelong Redskins fan, this causes me an enormous amount of pain and suffering. I can only guess this stems from some genetic disorder or organic mutation and I pray a cure is found in my lifetime. Until then, I am forced to suffer through and try and treat them as if they were normal people.

I have to confess that a large percentage of my free time at work over the years has been spent razzing the kitchen staff about how bad the Cowboys suck. One of my favorite things to do at the Freedom Steakhouse and Brewery when punching in a food order was to modify it slightly and manually type in *Dallas Blows* with my chicken wings for table 98.

If the customers only knew the fun we sometimes have with their food tickets.

Aside from the Cowboys thing, most of the kitchen staff are good eggs. That doesn't mean they don't have their moments.

For one thing, chefs tend to be particularly hot-headed. Walking into a kitchen during a busy dinner rush and asking an angry chef for a side of broccoli can be a harrowing experience. In some cases, it can take precious years off your life.

One day, I was working a day shift at the Big Digs. The bar was slow, but the restaurant got a pretty good lunch pop. Some guy ordered a cheeseburger.

I knew it would take a little bit, so I had one of the She Devils watch the bar while I went down and took a quick break. After my break, I made my way back by the kitchen to pick up my food. It wasn't ready.

"What are you waiting for?" the cook asked me.

I told him I was waiting on a cheeseburger.

"You just rang that shit in!" he screamed at me.

"Actually," I replied. "I rang it in a while ago. In fact, I went downstairs and took a break before I came up to get it."

This did not sit well with our cook. Apparently, he'd been having his ass handed to him for the last hour and had just caught up. My little cheeseburger turned out to be the straw that broke the camel's back.

I'm not sure I've ever witnessed a tirade like that, in all my years in the business. He was screaming and cussing, calling me this name and that, ranting on at how badly I was screwing up his mojo. At one point, he began yelling how he was going to jump across the line and kick my ass.

Really? You want to have a fist-fight over a cheeseburger?

I kept my cool, as best I could. Finally, I said, "Look, if you want to fight over a burger, we can do that later. Right now, I just need a burger for a guy who has been waiting fifteen minutes."

He calmed down and cooked my burger. After that, we were fine. I guess he just snapped. It happens.

When I worked at The Crustacean House, we had a brutally angry chef. He would fly off the handle over the slightest things. Most of the staff avoided contact with him unless absolutely necessary. There were people there who refused to speak to him or ever look him in the eye. The thing is, outside of work, he was a heck of a nice guy. I can only imagine it's that hot grill cooking your brain for eight hours a night.

Other than the occasional tirade, though, most of the kitchen staff are pretty down-to-earth and likable people. I do tend to keep my hand on my wallet when I'm around them, though. Just in case.

Besides, we all love the kitchen. It's our fortress of solitude. It's where we can go to cuss and yell, blowing off steam after we've been reamed out by some customer over a tuna fish sandwich. It's also the source of all that free food we love so much.

Since I've taken the time to talk about the kitchen, I suppose I should take a moment to mention the managers in our business.

These bozos are the bottom of the barrel. I'm just kidding. Most of them are terrific people and highly professional. Some I would not trust to wash my car. Many of them have become my close friends over the years. Some of them, not so much.

Sometimes, you will find people working as managers in restaurants because they are just not good enough to make it as bartenders and servers. Rather than count on making money based on their skill levels, they are forced to take the guaranteed money management positions offer.

Again, this is not always the case. Some people go into management because they truly aspire to climb the corporate ladder and wish to achieve greater levels of success. This is not a bad plan, as general managers can make very good money. It's just that getting to that level can be pretty rough. Mid- and lower-level managers tend to get paid more on the lines of teachers and police officers. In other words, they are vastly under paid. They are also forced to work ridiculous hours.

I have given thought to going into management myself, but I can't take the pay cut. Maybe someday, but chances are, if this book ever makes it to print, I can forget about that idea. I will be lucky to end up making drinks at a snowball stand on the boardwalk.

Aside from those genuinely good people who go into management for the right reasons, let's take a look at the other kind of people management jobs attract. The power-hungry, authority-seeking glory hounds who get erections when they tell people what to do. These are the kinds of people who will tell people what to do just for the satisfaction of seeing them do it.

Have you ever heard of the Little Hitler Complex? Sometimes they call it the Little Napoleon Complex. This is where short people make themselves feel bigger by ordering other people around. You see this all the time in the restaurant business. And they don't have to be short, either.

Don't get me wrong, I have known many wonderful people (and managers) who were vertically challenged. Being short in stature does not automatically make you a bad person and being taller doesn't make you a good one.

We had a manager at the Crustacean House who comes to mind. He looked like he was twelve and we all called him Doogie Howser behind his back. He was a snide little bastard who would go out of his way to show people he was in charge.

Doogie Howser would do anything to show how powerful he was. I once saw him fire a guy in the middle of a busy summer shift after the server asked him to take an iced tea to one of his tables. Doogie dropped off the glass of tea and went right to the computer to check and see if it had been rung up. The guy was really busy (which is why he asked Doogie to drop it off) and he hadn't had time to ring it in yet. Doogie fired him on the spot.

Doogie used to go around to all the sugar caddies on the tables and if there was one sugar packet out of place, he would dump them out so the server had to do it again from scratch. It was very junior high, which I guess was fitting for a 32-year-old dwarf with bad complexion.

I understand there are procedures that need to be followed in any business, and expecting your people to do their jobs correctly is not a bad thing. I am just not a big fan of treating adults like they are children. I believe if you want people to act professionally, you should treat people professionally. Nothing pisses me off quite as much as being treated like a 5-year-old.

There are management styles that lend themselves to this kind of behavior, and I have known people who use intimidation as a method for results, but it's been my experience that this seldom works. It takes a certain personality type to pull this off without looking like a total boob.

We had one GM at the Freedom Steakhouse and Brewery who pulled it off pretty well, but he was one of the few I've ever seen do it. It was actually pretty funny to witness.

The guy ran a pretty tight ship, and three quarters of the staff were terrified of him. He never really yelled or screamed a lot. He hardly ever fired anyone unless it was absolutely necessary, and he never made any sort of outrageous demands on his staff. He just wanted things done the way he wanted them done.

The personality he liked to portray to the staff was somewhere between John Wayne and Clint Eastwood, and many of his employees were afraid to speak to him. I knew people who had worked for him for years and never spoke more than a few words to him.

The funniest part of this was, when you actually took the time to get to know him, he was a pretty good guy.

Intimidation for the sake of intimidation does nothing if you don't have the respect factor to back it up, and that's probably why it worked for him. In many cases, the people who operate like this and think they are commanding the respect of those around them are merely looked upon as clowns by everyone in the workplace. Right, Doogie?

There are managers who think nothing of the people who work

under them and see people as a means to reach their sales goals and propel themselves to higher levels of success. This is a shame, but I have serious doubts that this is exclusive to our particular business.

Unfortunately, I have known many managers who think like this. I truly believe some of these people would love to keep all of his or her restaurant employees upstairs and unpaid in a barracks-like area until a customer walks in the door. At this point, an alarm would go off, complete with emergency lights and sirens, and we would rush over to the fireman's pole, slide down, and clock in before greeting our guests with a friendly smile. If some of these jokers could figure out a way to make this work, they would do it in a heartbeat.

That said, most of the managers I've known over the years are decent people just trying to make a living. For the most part, if they are good, we all work together as a team to get the job done.

It seems simple, but there are those who don't get it.

Have I left anybody out?

I've spent a good portion of this book ragging on the people who are our customers (for good reason), but as I said way back in Chapter One, the bad ones are greatly outnumbered by the good ones. Maybe it's time I gave some of them their due.

For as long as I have worked in bars and restaurants, there have been those people who have separated themselves from the masses. Some of them have gone on to become close friends while others have remained casual acquaintances. You would be surprised at the quality of people you can meet in a gin mill.

There are some who I see socially outside of work and there are some who I see socially at work. There are some whose names I don't even know and others whose family histories I could recite to you. There are people who have been to my home and I theirs, and there are people who travel down to Myrtle Beach three times a year and I have no idea where it even is they're from.

Some of these people have brought me gifts and magazine articles and apple pies and countless other things, and there are others who bring me nothing more than a smile and a friendly word.

I have listened to their problems and opinions and more jokes than I could ever remember and they have sat back and listened to mine and I know that I am a richer person for knowing them all.

Some of these people I see almost daily and others I see rarely. Some of my favorites I will likely never see again, but I will always hold out hope that our paths will cross somewhere down the line.

I have repeatedly used the word family throughout this book, and it applies to these people as much as it does to anyone I have ever worked alongside. These are the people who the words "customer" or "guest" don't seem to apply to and only the word "friend" could be used to describe them. Well, friend or family.

Way back in Chapter One I said that I was going to try and come up with the major question that my non-travel, non-adventure, travel-adventure story would try to answer. It was a question that I was still searching for and one that remained a mystery to me up to this point. Maybe I couldn't see it because it was staring me in the face the entire time.

Maybe the question is: What is it that has kept me showing up for work all these years? Why am I still doing this?

It's certainly not the most glamorous job out there. There are easier ways to make a living. The work can be brutal and difficult, and if you enter this field you are expected to pull your weight, sometimes more.

We don't much care for excuses in this business. You're judged every day on your performance, and sick days are for extreme emergencies, because when you don't show up someone else has to pick up your slack.

This job exposes the kind of person you are, and the rewards can be great and they can be disappointing and very often you won't know which until it's over. It can be fast or slow or overwhelming and frustrating. It can be sad and depressing one minute and the next thing you know you can be giggling like a little kid.

If nothing else, it's not sitting in a cubicle.

For me, I guess it's just where I fit. At least, it's where I fit until I decide what it is that I want to do with my life, and I'm okay with that.

I make no apologies for the choices I've made. There have been plenty of mistakes along the way and probably many things I should have done differently, but who can't say that about their lives? In the end, it's just a chapter in my journey and it's a chapter I wouldn't rewrite for anything. Part of me feels like it was the journey I was meant to take.

Before undertaking this project, I had written a handful of

novels. Three have actually made it to print and have achieved a moderate amount of success. I even have a decent and loyal following for my mystery books, believe it or not. I might not be Stephen King, but I'm having a lot of fun with it.

Many times after someone reads one of my books, they will come back to me and ask me where I come up with the odd assortment of characters that I write about. I've never had a really good answer to this question before, but after writing this book, I think I can see where the inspiration came from. Maybe that was why I was meant to take this journey.

And that brooding question that I was trying to answer along the way? What was it that brought me to this place and kept me doing this for all this time? I think I've been answering it all along. I've answered it with every story. I've answered it with every joke.

It seems so simple to me now.

It's the people.

The bad ones and the pains-in-the-ass and even the ones who drive me crazy, they all have their place in the puzzle. Without them, what would I have to laugh about with the good ones? Because, in the end, it is the good ones who kept me coming back for more. They are the ones who make me love what I do, even when I hate it.

I have been very lucky to be surrounded by so many of these people over the years, and I wouldn't trade a single minute that I've had with any of them for anything in the world. They are not only who this book is for but, in the end, what it's really all about.

One time I was working my shift at the Freedom Steakhouse and a girl I work with (Tara) was preparing a bunch of drinks for her table. It was more than she could carry and she turned to me and asked if I had and extra hand. I told her "no" but that I did have a cousin who had six toes on one foot.

Some time later, this same evil genius of a girl was waiting on a table with kids. They had one of those Mr. Potato Heads and when they left they forgot some of the pieces. One of those pieces was a long, thin arm with a white, gloved hand on it. She stashed it away and waited for just the right moment.

Weeks later, I was working with her and I had a particularly large table. I couldn't carry all the drinks and turned to her and asked (stupid me), "Do you have an extra hand?"

"As a matter of fact, I do," she said with a smile, reaching into her pocket and handing me the little plastic hand.

It's just the goofy stuff like that I remember most.

A few years ago, REO Speedwagon was playing a concert in Myrtle Beach. A few of the older bartenders at the Freedom Steakhouse and Brewery were talking about going to the show.

We worked with a younger girl who overheard the conversation and she interrupted to ask, "Who is Oreo Speedwagon?"

They're the people who deliver the cookies.

You may or may not find this next one funny, but I love this story. I have this friend who works as a manager at an Italian restaurant in town. He had thrown out his back and he was in misery. One of his coworkers went out to his car and got him one of those back braces that you wear under your shirt for extra support.

Scott (another Scott) didn't want to put it on, but he figured it was worth a shot. The night is going on and he has this thing on under his shirt. The brace is helping and everything is hunky dory, and Scott is seating a couple at their table when the guy reaches out and touches him on the side, right where the top of the back brace ends.

At this point, both men freeze in place and they look at each other with awkward, shocked glares. Scott told me that he just knew that the guy thought he was wearing some kind of corset under there. He wanted to tell the guy what was going on but at that point there just wasn't a way to bring it up. We call that one the "man girdle story."

You can't buy entertainment like that.

Years ago, when I worked at Freedom, an unfortunate decision on my part yielded me a black eye. That same week, one of our assistant managers was jumped, and he received a black eye. About that time, they had hired a new server who also happened to have a black eye.

A few of us were sitting at the end of the bar after our shift with our GM. Our assistant manager walked by. A few moments later, the new server walked by. My buddy, Brian, looked up at me, then turned to our GM.

"I get it, Chris," he said. "First rule of fight club is, there is no fight club."

I love that one.

Another day a lady was sitting at my bar and perusing the menu. She called me over and asked, "What kind of beans do they use in the black bean dip?"

Jelly beans, but just the black ones.

What kind of beans do you think they use in the black bean dip? Is it called lima bean dip? Green bean dip? Pinto bean dip?

The insanity never stops. What are you going to do?

Welcome to my world.

I hope you enjoyed the journey.

And, by the way, if you have ever been in one of the bars or restaurants where I have worked and you are reading my book and thought maybe you recognized yourself in one of my stories ... sorry. It's all in fun. No hard feelings.

So the next time you find yourself in your favorite watering hole or eatery and your bartender or server asks if they can get you anything, take it easy on them. There is an excellent chance that person is a good friend of mine, so do me a favor and treat them the way you'd like me to treat a friend of yours.

It's as simple as that.

The End

(But not really)

THE BARTENDER AND SERVER APTITUDE TEST
OR
THE BSATS

Let's see how much you've learned.

1. You have just finished having dinner at one of your favorite restaurants. The food and service were wonderful and you couldn't be happier. You should:

    a. Tip a minimum of 15 percent.

    b. Leave a shiny quarter and call it a day.

    c. Save some money and leave a verbal tip in lieu of cash.

    d. Pay with a credit card, making sure to leave a fat tip, but taking both copies of the credit card slip with you when you leave.

2. You are eating in a more upscale restaurant than your usual fast food stop. At your place setting are two forks. The outside fork is for:

    a. In case you drop the other one.

    b. Eating with both hands.

    c. Defending yourself against the charging hordes

    d. Salad.

3. If you order a steak in a restaurant and it comes out over-cooked, you should:

    a. Berate your server like they assaulted your mother.

    b. Scream, cry, and pantomime stabbing yourself in the chest with an invisible knife.

    c. Man up and eat it anyway.

    d. Alert your server so they can have a new steak prepared for you.

4. If you walk into a restaurant and there are ten empty tables, but one of them is dirty, you should:

    a. Choose any of the clean tables.

    b. Call the Table Police.

    c. Sit at the dirty table and complain to a manager.

    d. Take the dirty table and scrounge through the leftovers for food scraps.

5. You walk into a busy restaurant in the peak of the season. The hostess tells you it will be a 45-minute wait. You should:

    a. Hold your breath until they agree to sit you.

    b. Demand compensation for pain and suffering.

    c. Find a small family, overpower them, and take their table.

    d. Decide to either wait the 45 minutes or go somewhere else.

6. You receive your check after dining in your favorite restaurant. After inspecting it, you feel you were charged for items you didn't order. You should:

   a. Hold your server in a headlock until they take the charges off your bill.

   b. Dine and dash.

   c. Fake a heart attack.

   d. Point the mistake out to your server so they can fix the problem.

7. Your server drops off your bowl of soup and you discover a dead fly floating in it. You should:

   a. Curse the high heavens.

   b. Enjoy the extra and FREE boost of protein.

   c. Accuse your server of planting it there in an attempt to ruin your life.

   d. Tell your server so they can replace it with a fresh bowl.

8. Your server brings you a glass of wine and you notice there is lipstick on the rim. You should:

   a. Smash the top of the glass against the table edge and use the jagged edges to attack your server.

   b. Go through the room and try to match the lipstick shade with one of the women dining.

   c. Lick it off and drink it anyway.

   d. Point it out to your server so they can get you a fresh glass.

9. If you go into a restaurant and your server or bartender is cheerful and polite, they are most likely:

    a. Whacked out on Ritalin.

    b. Mentally handicapped.

    c. A member of some bizarre cult.

    d. A professional who understands how to do their job.

10. If your dinner is taking a particularly long time, it probably means:

    a. Your server hates you.

    b. The kitchen staff is out back getting stoned.

    c. There is a nationwide conspiracy against you.

    d. You ordered your steak well done.

11. If you are the kind of person who complains constantly about every little thing in hopes of getting free shit, you can expect:

    a. Free shit.

    b. To taste a lot of spit in your lifetime.

    c. An overdue visit from karma.

12. If you are a bartender or server and someone complains about his or her meal, you should:

    a. Act like you don't speak English.

    b. Blame the kitchen.

    c. Challenge them to a duel.

    d. Get it fixed and get on with your life.

13. Your bartender or server is there to:

    a. Make fun of.

    b. Serve out a judge ordered penal sentence.

    c. Be your whipping boy.

    d. Fetch you stuff.

14. Your average bar or restaurant is there to:

    a. Swindle you out of every last penny they can.

    b. Give you an assortment of people to yell at.

    c. Feed your growing paranoia.

    d. Provide you with goods and services.

15. It's a busy Saturday night at your favorite watering hole and the bartender is slammed. When he takes your order, you should:

    a. Tell him or her about your Uncle Henry's hemorrhoid operation.

    b. Begin listing all the things you don't like to drink.

    c. Complain about the lack of elbow room.

    d. Order a drink.

16. A train leaves the station at 2:30, heading west. Another train, heading east, leaves at three. When does your bartender or server wish you were under one of these trains?

    a. When you complain because the ranch dressing isn't ranchy enough.

    b. When your never-ending story is keeping them from their other customers.

    c. When, while screaming in their face because your well-done burger is dry, you are pelting them with specks of food and spittle

    d. Um, I was told there would be no math questions on this test.

17. If your bartender or server asks if you would like a drink, a proper response is:

    a. What's the frequency, Kenneth?

    b. I have a bunion on my foot the size of a quarter.

    c. Hmm, what am I in the mood for?

    d. A vodka and tonic, please.

18. Your favorite restaurant closes at 10 p.m. You show up at 9:58 p.m. You should:

    a. Kick off your shoes and announce, "We're going to be here a while."

    b. Make sure to take an extra twenty minutes to peruse the menu before ordering.

    c. Order a three-course dinner and enjoy your spit-drizzled meal.

    d. Go to another restaurant that stays open later.

19. The best thing about being a bartender or server is:

    a. Apologizing for stuff that isn't your fault.

    b. Being yelled at by a man with a mouthful of potato salad.

    c. All the free table scraps.

    d. The buildup of antibodies in your system from all the germs you touch.

20. A guy walks into your bar with a parrot on his shoulder. You should:

    a. Assume he is not there to meet friends.

    b. Accept the fact your life has become a bad bar joke.

    c. Prepare to clean up a lot of bird poop.

    d. Treat him as you would anyone else.

21. The first rule of the restaurant business is:

    a. The customer is seldom right.

    b. He who smelt it dealt it.

    c. Don't get crabs on the crabs.

    d. Gas, ass, or grass, nobody rides for free.

22. A sure sign that your server or bartender is having a bad day is:

    a. The profanity-laced tirade you hear coming from the kitchen.

    b. The painful and strained look in their eyes as they attempt to keep smiling.

    c. The way they are white-knuckling their ballpoint pen as you read them back the menu like it was bedtime story.

    d. The mere fact they are at work and not someplace cool.

23. You are a server working the dinner shift when someone complains his steak is overcooked. You should:

    a. Point out that there are starving children in the world who would kill for an overcooked steak.

    b. Repeat everything they say in the form of a question.

    c. Offer up one of your kidneys as compensation for their pain and suffering.

    d. Apologize, even though it isn't your fault, and get them another steak.

24. Your bartender or server loves it when you:

    a. Treat them like they were the monkey boy at the carnival freak show.

    b. Shovel as much food into your pie hole as you can before asking for a refill of your sweet tea.

    c. Assume they have the IQ of a used tire.

    d. Treat them as you would like to be treated.

25. If you enjoyed this book:

    a. You are, obviously, an intelligent person with a great sense of humor.

    b. You should buy copies to give as gifts to all your friends and family.

    c. You should recommend it to everyone you know.

    d. All of the above.

Thanks for reading

"Life Behind Bars"

If you enjoyed this book, please tell a friend.

Also, if you have time, leave a review on Amazon. You have no idea how important Amazon reviews are to a small book like this. Good, bad, or somewhere in the middle, they make a huge difference. All reviews welcome.

Feel free to check out our website at www.lastcallpress.com for all the latest information on what we have going on. There's a lot on tap in the upcoming months, so be sure to check back often.

Do you have your own crazy, zany, funny story about working in the service industry? We'd love to hear it. Go to our site at www.lastcallpress.com and follow the link to the Life Behind Bars Message Board to share your story, or use the contact link to send it to us directly. We can't wait to hear what you've got. Feel free to contact us with anything. We're always looking for suggestions, opinions, and anything else you want to throw our way.

OTHER BOOKS FROM

LAST CALL PRESS

The Ocean Forest

By Troy D. Nooe

(Shamus Award Finalist)

Frankie McKeller hates the beach. He has ever since that day on the one they call Omaha. If the guy who saved his life during the war wasn't getting married, he'd never have made the trip to Myrtle Beach, South Carolina. As a low-budget gumshoe out of Baltimore, he isn't prepared for a weekend hobnobbing with the Southern elite. When a prominent wedding guest is found dead, the six-week course he took in private investigation proves lacking, as well. Frankie is out of his element at the exclusive Ocean Forest Hotel, snooping and stumbling his way through his first-ever murder case. The deeper he wades in, the murkier things get, and Frankie is forced to face his own ghosts and demons. It's a three-day stay in murder and betrayal in this Shamus Award-nominated book.

Damn Yankee

By Troy D. Nooe

Frankie McKeller is back on the beach, this time as the house detective at the exclusive Ocean Forest Hotel. When asked to look into the disappearance of a young girl, he is thrown into an underworld of bootleggers, illegal gambling, and vice. When a second girl is found dead in the sand, all bets are off, and Frankie finds himself trying to put the pieces together in two crimes as he struggles to save the life of a missing young girl and avenge the death of another. It's murder and mayhem on the beach as Frankie contends with the other side of life in Myrtle Beach and a taboo romance that can never be.

Southern noir served beach style in this second installment of The Frankie McKeller Mystery Series.

Long-Legged Rosie

By Troy D. Nooe

Baltimore trouble follows Frankie McKeller to the beach in the person of Rosie, a doll with a history as long as her fabulous gams. Does she need Frankie's help in escaping an abusive mobster boyfriend or is she using him for her own devices? Is a U.S. senator a lecherous abuser of power or the victim of a plot to undermine his reputation and his political future? Myrtle Beach is the backdrop for a series of murders and intrigue, and once again, Frankie's future and well-being are on the line. It's the third novel in the Frankie McKeller Mystery Series and things are heating up in the summer sun of old-time Myrtle Beach.

Five Kinds of Nothing

By Troy D. Nooe

(ebook exclusive)

It's five mini-adventures featuring Frankie and other characters from the Frankie McKeller Mystery Series. Check out these five new and original tales, plus two bonus stories, as Frankie and friends cross paths with a delectable party girl with ulterior motives, a raging biker with an axe to grind, a lost veteran looking for revenge, and much, much more.

It's a great introduction to the Frankie McKeller Mystery Series or just enough action and intrigue to get you by until the next Frankie novel comes out.

Win a Chance to get Killed Off

In a Future Frankie McKeller Mystery Novel

Now is your chance to get bumped off in a future Frankie McKeller Mystery. It's free, simple and relatively painless. Just drop us a line and tell us why you should be a murder victim in a future Frankie McKeller book. Author Troy D. Nooe will be selecting at least one person to be featured and knocked off in the next Murder in Myrtle Beach novel and we want that person to be YOU. Send us and email with, "Kill Me Off" in the subject line to: lastcallpress@gmail.com and tell us why you deserve to die in print or go to www.lastcallpress.com.

The author reserves the right to decide the method of your demise, but if you have something in mind, go ahead and throw it out there. Who knows?

The winner (or winners) will be notified prior to the release of the next book and his or her name will be posted on the website with a proper eulogy.

www.lastcallpress.com

www.ingramcontent.com/pod-product-compliance
Lightning Source LLC
LaVergne TN
LVHW051505080426
835509LV00017B/1932

9 780692 712054